PRAISE FOR *THE DOLLOP BOOK OF FROSTING*

"Heather's deliciously unique world of frosting makes for an absolutely delightful cookbook! It truly is a sweet treasure trove of 'must-have' recipes for anyone who loves to bake!"

—Linda Hundt, founder of Sweetie-licious and author of *Sweetie-licious Pies: Eat Pie, Love Life*

"Heather is a girl after my own heart. Her passion for inventiveness shines through in these easy-to-make sweet-treats recipes. Her frostings are out-of-this-world good and I can't wait to try more of them out on friends at future gatherings and dinner parties!"

—Kate Payne, author of *The Hip Girl's Guide to Homemaking*

~ The ~
DOLLOP
Book of Frosting

Sweet and Savory Icings, Spreads, Meringues,
and Ganaches for Dessert *and Beyond*

Heather "*Cupcakes*" Saffer

Avon, Massachusetts

Published by
Adams Media, a division of F+W Media, Inc.
57 Littlefield Street, Avon, MA 02322. U.S.A.
www.adamsmedia.com

ISBN 10: 1-4405-5883-3
ISBN 13: 978-1-4405-5883-2
eISBN 10: 1-4405-5884-1
eISBN 13: 978-1-4405-5884-9

Printed in the United States of America.

10 9 8 7 6 5 4 3 2 1

Library of Congress Cataloging-in-Publication Data

Saffer, Heather.
  The dollop book of frosting : sweet and savory icings, spreads, meringues, and ganaches
for dessert and beyond / Heather "Cupcakes" Saffer.
       pages cm
  Includes bibliographical references and index.
  ISBN-13: 978-1-4405-5883-2 (alkaline paper)
  ISBN-10: 1-4405-5883-3 (alkaline paper)
  ISBN-13: 978-1-4405-5884-9 (electronic)
  ISBN-10: 1-4405-5884-1 (electronic)
1. Icings, Cake. I. Title.
  TX771.2.S24 2013
  641.86'539--dc23
                            2013015204

Always follow safety and commonsense cooking protocol while using kitchen utensils, oper-
ating ovens and stoves, and handling uncooked food. If children are assisting in the prepara-
tion of any recipe, they should always be supervised by an adult.

Many of the designations used by manufacturers and sellers to distinguish their product are
claimed as trademarks. Where those designations appear in this book and F+W Media was
aware of a trademark claim, the designations have been printed with initial capital letters.

All Photos © Matt Wittmeyer Photography.

This book is available at quantity discounts for bulk purchases.
For information, please call 1-800-289-0963.

DEDICATION

To unabashed frosting lovers everywhere: Never stop fighting for that corner piece.

And to Mom and Dad: Thank you for always scraping off your own frosting so that I could have more.

ACKNOWLEDGMENTS

Let's give these people a round of applause (or a round of frosting and drinks)!

Mom: You didn't teach me how to bake but you did support everything I set out to do. You're the best box folder in town and the only friend I've ever needed. Thank you.

Dad: Thank you for teaching me how to be an adult. I promise I'll catch on one of these days.

Grandma: When you loved my frosting, that's when I knew it was really good.

Randy: Who knew you were a talented mascot maker and crowd tamer? A skilled and caring brother—score!

Dan: It's because of you that this book is in your hands. Thank you for believing in me, encouraging me, and tolerating my persistent screams about everything. You are more than wonderful.

Michele and Jason: Thank you for finding me, believing in me, and giving me a chance. Sometimes I want to start conversations with "my agents" just so I can tell people how awesome you are.

Halli, Katie, and the whole Adams Media team: Thank you for believing in my crazy love of frosting and for taming my spastic thoughts into one cohesive and fabulous book!

Brando: That summer. That weekend. That day. Thank you.

Jason: For burgers and bitching and everything in between.

Chris, Steve, Tim, Ron, Michelle, and the entire Monroe County CrossFit team: If it weren't for you, my pants would never fit again and I'd be beating people up all over town. Thank you for keeping me fit and sane while I shove my face with frosting.

To every customer who has followed me through my many changes, your loyalty has never been overlooked. Thank you.

To my Facebook fans, Twitter followers, blog readers, frosting lovers, and you there holding this book! Thank you. Thank you for reading this book, baking from this book, and savoring Dollop's frostings. It's your love and support that inspires me to keep on creating sweet things. Please never stop.

And to the others: May this book inspire you to one day be sweet.

CONTENTS

Introduction   8
The Tricks of the Trade   11

PART 1: THE CLASSICS 17

VANILLA BUTTERCREAM 18
  Vanilla Cupcakes 20

CHOCOLATE BUTTERCREAM 21
  Chocolate Cupcakes 23

CREAM CHEESE FROSTING 24
  Red Velvet Cupcakes 26

STRAWBERRY FROSTING 27
  Strawberry-Frosted Limoncello "Shortcakes" 29

SALTED CARAMEL FROSTING 30
  Salted Caramel Apple Tarts 32

MINT CHOCOLATE CHIP FROSTING 33
  Mint Chocolate Cookie Trifle 35

CW PEANUT BUTTER BUTTERCREAM 36
  Ultimate Dude Peanut Butter Cookie
  Dough Cupcakes 38

LEMON GLAZE FROSTING 40
  Frosting Fruit Salad 41

COOKIES AND CREAM FROSTING 43
  Cookies and Cream Ice Cream Trifle 44

PEPPERMINT BUTTERCREAM 46
  Peppermint Cookie Cups with
  Peppermint Ice Cream 47

MOCHA FROSTING 49
  Mocha Upside-Down Cupcakes 50

RASPBERRY BUTTERCREAM 51
  Spinach "Salad" 53

S'MORE FROSTING 54
  S'more Push-Pop Parfaits 56

PART 2: WITH A TWIST 57

CW BROWN SUGAR FROSTING 58
  Sweet Potato Fries and Blueberry
  Ketchup Cupcakes 60

COOKIE DOUGH FROSTING 63
  Chocolate Chip Cookie Wafers 64

TOFFEE HONEY FROSTING 65
  Frosted Popcorn 66

BANANAS FOSTER FROSTING 68
  Bananas Foster Cupcake-Pancake Bites 69

CHOCOLATE STRAWBERRY
CREAM CHEESE FROSTING 71
  Banana Split Cake Balls 72

PUMPKIN SPICE CREAM CHEESE FROSTING 73
  Pumpkin Spice Pizzas 75

TOFFEE GANACHE FROSTING 76
  Coffee Toffee Ganache Frosting Truffles 77

HAZELNUT COFFEE FROSTING 79
  Vanilla Hazelnut Coffee Pudding 80

BROWNIE BATTER FROSTING 81
   Salted Triple Chocolate Brownie Batter Cookies . . 83

GINGERSNAP STOUT FROSTING 84
   Gingersnap Stout Pie 85

CHOCOLATE CHIPOTLE FROSTING 87
   Chocolate Chipotle Frosted Nachos with Chili 88

MALBEC GANACHE FROSTING 89
   Chocolate Raspberry Pasta 91

STRAWBERRY MERINGUE FROSTING 92
   Floating Strawberry Meringue Drop Cookies 94

MARGARITA MERINGUE FROSTING 95
   Margarita Crispy Rice Treats 97

STRAWBERRY CHAMPAGNE FROSTING 98
   Champagne Cake Bites with Raspberries 100

PART 3: BE CRAZY: LIVE
A FROSTED LIFE 101

LAVENDER ORANGE FROSTING 102
   Lavender Orange Biscotti 104

HONEY BRIE FROSTING 105
   Rosemary Sea Salt Shortbreads with Fig 107

WHITE CHOCOLATE BLUEBERRY GANACHE 108
   Pear Cookies 110

ORANGE CARDAMOM ICING 111
   Orange Cut-Out Cookies 113

CW CLOVE BUTTERCREAM 114
   Bittersweet Chocolate, Clove, Beer,
   and Spicy Beer Caramel Cupcakes 116

STRAWBERRY BALSAMIC GOAT
CHEESE FROSTING 118
   Strawberry Spinach Cheesecakes 120

JUNIPER CHOCOLATE FROSTING 121
   Blackberry Brownies 123

PEACH BASIL WHIPPED CREAM 124
   Peach Basil Pancakes 126

CASHEW SRIRACHA FROSTING 127
   Sriracha Brownies 129

COCONUT ALMOND FROSTING 130
   Cashew Chocolate Bacon Bark 131

TAHINI CURRANT FROSTING 133
   Tahini Currant Crispy Rice Bars 134

PISTACHIO COCONUT FROSTING 135
   Pistachio Coconut Cookie Thins 137

HONEY MUSTARD FROSTING 138
   Corn Dog Cupcakes 140

CHEDDAR BACON FROSTING 141
   Cheddar Beer-Boiled Pretzels 143

CW CINNAMON WHISKY BUTTERCREAM 144
   Strawberry Firebomb Cupcakes 146

CONCORD GRAPE FROSTING 149
   Peanut Butter Granola 150

MAPLE BACON FROSTING 151
   Vanilla Buttermilk Waffles 152

Appendix: Conversion Chart   154
Index   155

INTRODUCTION

Ever had S'more Frosting? Honey Mustard Frosting? A frosting that tastes just like gingersnap stout? Have you had hot Vanilla Buttermilk Waffles slathered with fresh Maple Bacon Frosting? Or a scrumptious fruit salad topped with a creamy Lemon Glaze Frosting? No?

Well, it sounds like *The Dollop Book of Frosting* might just change your life! Throughout this book you'll find forty-five frosting recipes for classics like Vanilla Buttercream; unusual frostings with a twist like Chocolate Chipotle Frosting; and crazy, out-of-the-box frosting flavors like Cheddar Bacon Frosting, Tahini Currant Frosting, and Cashew Sriracha Frosting.

"Why frosting?" you ask. "Isn't that just something you put on something else as an afterthought?" Absolutely not! Although frosting can double as spreads for cupcakes, pies, pretzels, popcorn, and even salads—see the forty-five supplemental recipes paired with each frosting if you need proof—it's also pretty amazing on its own. After all, it's a fact that many frosting lovers sneak to the fridge in the middle of the night and secretly grab a spoonful of frosting, praying they don't get caught. How do I know? Well, let's just say that frosting has played a main role in how I came to find not only my calling in life but my center.

My name is Heather "Cupcakes" Saffer, but most people just call me Cupcakes, a nickname for which I consider myself fortunate (living in New York you tend to meet plenty of people with interesting nicknames, and I think Cupcakes beats Jimmy the Chin any day). Today, I tend to think of a cupcake as just an FDV (Frosting Delivery Vehicle), but cupcakes have played a big role in my life. Back in 2008, I opened a cupcake business, the Cupcake Dreamery, and after the Dreamery closed, I opened Dollop Gourmet Cupcake Creations—a cupcake bar located in the heart of Rochester, New York. When I started Dollop in 2010, buoyed by a ton of enthusiastic and supportive press, I auditioned for the Food Network's *Cupcake Wars*. I wasn't chosen, but in 2011 *Cupcake Wars* called again with a second chance at an audition. This time I made the cut.

I always said that I would put my cupcakes up against anyone's, anywhere. On *Cupcake Wars* I did just that. And you know what? I won! The frostings that I created on the show were a major reason that I took home the win, and you'll find a variety of those recipes—including the Clove Buttercream, Brown Sugar Frosting, and Peanut Butter Buttercream—along with the recipes for the winning cupcakes throughout the book marked with this *Cupcake Wars* icon.

But even though I "live" cupcakes, I love frosting, and in 2012, I closed Dollop Gourmet Cupcake Creations to open Dollop Gourmet, a frosting company that has recently created a line of all-natural, gluten-free, dairy-free, *and* vegan ready-to-eat frostings that are crazy delicious and coming soon to a supermarket near you.

It's a big change, but over the years, my philosophy for baking and living is basically that the best part of the cupcake is what you put on top of it. So start whipping up these little bowls of sugary heaven—and remember: It's what you dollop your life with that really matters. Enjoy!

The
TRICKS *of the* TRADE

Throughout my years of frosting making, researching, and perfecting, I've learned a lot about how to make the fluffiest, creamiest frosting and how to avoid ending up with a dead bowl of clumpy, unusable buttered sugar. Frosting can be heavenly delicious and fantastically fun to make, especially if you have the correct tools and follow some of my "swear by" tricks in order to avoid the doldrums of trial and error. You'll find this info in this part along with some baking tips for making the best FDVs that you can . . . because, no matter how much you may want to, you can't *always* eat frosting with your fingers! So take a read through, check your cupboards, hit the store, and use this section for reference as you work through each delicious recipe!

What You'll Need to Dig Up (or Out)

I don't like buying tools, and I'm not a gadget freak. I'm actually a minimalist at heart, and one of the best things about making frosting—and all the other delicious recipes that you'll find throughout the book—is that it's not super complicated. You probably have a lot of the items on the following list in your kitchen already, and if not, they're easy to find. Take some time to take stock of what you have—and buy what you don't—before you end up wrist-deep in frosting. I tend to make many runs to the grocery store, but you can avoid this by always having the basics on hand. Or you can do as I do and bake above a bar—with a willing errand-running assistant by your side. Try not to yell at your assistant, and always bribe him or her with the finished frosting-filled product at the end. After all, once you get an idea of how delicious your frosting is going to be, you don't want anything holding you up!

+ Alcohol: beer (stouts, porters, ales), wine, tequila, Cointreau, your favorite alcohol of choice
+ Brownie pans: 8" × 8" and 9" × 13"
+ Candy thermometer: You'll need this to cook caramel to make sure it hits the right temperature.
+ Cookie sheets
+ Cooling racks
+ Cupcake tins: mini and standard size
+ Food processor: I swear by my Ninja Express Chop food chopper, in fact, I have three. They're cheap, reliable, and fast. You'll be chopping lots of things, so do yourself a major favor and get one.

+ Ice cream scoops: You'll need a standard size scoop and a mini scoop for truffles and cookies.
+ Knives, forks, and spoons: You'll need all kinds of knives, but if you have a butcher block of knives, then you surely have everything you need. You'll also need forks to eat the food and spoons to scoop and taste.
+ Measuring cups and spoons: Glass, metal, or plastic—whichever you fancy, make sure you have a full set each of cups and spoons. If you have multiple sets, that's even better as it will save you time on dish washing as you go.
+ Music: Baking is always better with music.
+ Nonstick cooking spray
+ Parchment paper and wax paper: These are not the same things. Wax paper has a coating that is not meant for use in the oven whereas parchment paper is the perfect baking tray liner for oven usage. Most of the time you'll be using parchment paper, so invest in a couple of rolls.
+ Pie pans: 8" or 9" for large pies or mini pans for individual pies. You can even use disposable foil pans.
+ Piping bags or Ziploc bags
+ Push-pop containers: Remember the old-school ice cream containers? You can buy them online or at Target.
+ Ramekins or custard dishes
+ Scissors for cutting tips off pastry bags
+ Spatulas: These will be some of your most useful tools for frosting, so start collecting them. You'll need long-handled spatulas to reach deep into the bowl, offset spatulas to spread, and flat spatulas with serrated edges for spreading and cutting.

- ✦ Stand mixer with paddle attachment and whisk attachment
- ✦ Toothpicks: These are extremely necessary in testing cakes and brownies while in the oven to make sure they're thoroughly baked.
- ✦ Trifle dishes

Hold That Whisk! Before You Frost . . .

I know it's tempting to jump right in; you can almost taste the creamy, fluffy frosting on your lips right now, can't you? I know I can! But it's important that you hold that whisk and focus on the loveliness you're about to create and learn some tips to make it the best it can be. So, take a few minutes here to read about the basics of frosting styles, softening butter, and the key to sugar addition. Once you learn the tricks of the trade, you'll be whipping up bowls of frosting masterpieces in no time!

Frosting Styles

Frosting comes in many different styles, including American buttercream (my personal favorite!), whipped cream, cream cheese frosting, icing, glaze, caramel, meringue, and ganache. Anything included in the book that doesn't fit into one of these categories is a Heather Cupcakes original!

Butter

Always use unsalted butter and always soften it to room temperature before you use it. If you forget to remove the butter from the fridge before you're ready (as I do 99 percent of the time), just microwave it for 20–30 seconds, keeping an eye on it to make sure it doesn't melt. If after 30 seconds it's not soft, flip it over and try again. You should only need to microwave it for a total of 40–60 seconds at most. Be warned: If you go too far and melt the butter, you can't use it for frosting anymore. So don't let it melt!

Powdered Sugar

I recommend using 10x powdered sugar (this is the finest grade and will usually be labeled as such right on the bag) because it's less likely to cause lumps in your frosting. If your sugar is lumpy, take a few extra minutes to sift it or run a whisk through it. Sifting tends to be time-consuming, but it's worth it. The same rule applies to cocoa powder. To keep lumps from forming in the first place, keep your sugar sealed tightly in an airtight container.

Some recipes call for several cups of powdered sugar, and if you're doubling or tripling the recipe, even more. Add the sugar to the bowl *slowly* or you will be covered in powdered sugar. I promise you on this one. Also, if you have a stand mixer, you'll want to switch back and forth from speed 1 to 2 very quickly after the initial addition of sugar to start the mixing process, otherwise the mixer will turn on too fast and the sugar will be mixed in your hair instead of mixed in the frosting. I have the pictures to prove it.

Salt

Sometimes I recommend coarse sea salt or fine sea salt in a recipe, but most of the time kosher salt or table salt is the preferable salt for frosting.

Whipping

When it comes to whipping frosting, when I say light and fluffy, I really mean light and fluffy. Just keep whipping that frosting, for 5 minutes and sometimes more. It's hard to overbeat buttercream, honestly. The more you whip it, the lighter it becomes. This doesn't mean that you should let the mixer go for half an hour—that would be getting carried away— but don't be afraid to give it some time. Typically I use the paddle attachment on my stand mixer, but you can also use the whisk attachment.

Blending

When making frosting, be sure to scrape down the sides and bottom of the mixing bowl after the addition of each ingredient. Everything needs to be well blended and well incorporated, and you can only ensure this by using a spatula to periodically scrape down the bowl.

Storage

If you're not using your frosting for a few days, store it in an airtight container in the fridge, and if you're keeping it for weeks, store it in the freezer. When the frosting comes out of the fridge or freezer, it always helps to bring it to room temperature and even to rewhip it to soften it before use. Frosting is always best when used fresh, but you'll be amazed at how well frosting comes back to life with just a little fresh whipping.

Baking

You don't want to waste the frosting you made by burning your brownies or overcooking your cupcakes. To make sure your baked goods are the per- fect level of done, stick a toothpick in the center of cakes and brownies, then remove it, checking to see if gooey batter is stuck to it. If it looks like batter, the cake or brownie is not yet fully baked; check it again in a couple minutes. If cake is stuck to the toothpick, you can remove the pan; it's at the perfect point. If the toothpick is bone dry, remove the pan from the oven right away as it may be over baked. But don't worry too much; you can always resurrect an over- done cupcake with frosting!

Decorating

This is not a cake-decorating book. I repeat: This is not a cake-decorating book. This book is chock full of amazingly unique and delicious frostings used in versatile and creative ways. These frostings are meant to taste good, not create roses or Hello Kitty logos. To decorate cakes and cookies, use a piping bag or a Ziploc bag with the corner cut off. You can also use spatulas, knives, the backs of spoons—really anything will do to spread your frosting in a pinch.

Fondant

I'm not a fan of fondant so you won't find any here other than in the recipe for the Ultimate Dude Peanut Butter Cookie Dough Cupcakes that I made on *Cupcake Wars*. And this is only because I needed to transform my chocolate chip cookie toppers into Monster Truck tires! Fondant does have its aesthetic uses at times.

Sweetness

Frosting almost always calls for sugar. The recipes found throughout this book are proven winners—as determined by *Cupcake Wars* and my customers alike. However, everyone has different standards and tolerances for sweetness, which is why it's key for you to taste as you go along, especially while adding sugar. Dip a spoon or a toothpick into your frosting in the middle of the sugar addition stage and use your intuition and taste buds to make sure it's the way you want it. If you've already gone and added too much sugar, add a little salt to counteract the sweet. It's hard to mess frosting up too badly, but stay tuned in as you go along. You can always add more sugar, but you can't take sugar out.

Yields

When I mention the yields for each frosting recipe, just know this might vary. If you're frosting cupcakes with a piping bag versus spreading the frosting with a knife, you'll be using more frosting and thus yielding less from the recipe. And, if you like more frosting (as I do) on your desserts and snacks, you'll also yield less frosting from each recipe. Feel free to halve, double, or triple each recipe according to the amount you want to yield and your own frosting preference.

As you go along, remember that you don't need to be perfect; your frosting doesn't need to look like it came from the pages of a magazine. If you frost cupcakes and transport them to a picnic on a 90°F day, they will melt. We're using real butter here, folks. If you drop frosted cupcakes, they will look like a mess—they're almost human like that. Frosting is fun, and above all, you must have fun while making it. Now get to it! Have fun, impress your friends, and be adventurous! I'll be with you every step of the way.

PART 1

~ The ~
CLASSICS

I was working as a car dealership cashier—another in a long string of hopeless dead-end jobs—when I saw "it": a light fluffy cloud of Vanilla Buttercream frosting in my head. Was I hungry? Maybe; it *was* past lunchtime. Was I bored? Definitely! I was desperate for any way out of my job. In that cloud, I saw a way to go into business for myself and escape my tedious, boring life.

There was one small problem: I didn't know how to cook. So I enrolled in Heather's Cooking School. My professors were Google and YouTube. In time, I perfected two basic frosting recipes without any formal cooking experience or background. Although the Internet taught me technique, it was my innate love for creamy American buttercream that taught me flair. Balancing the right amount of butter with the perfect pinch of salt and just the right amount of sugar became my goal—and achieve it I did. The classic frostings that you'll find in this part are fluffy, sweet piles of heaven that won't cloy at your taste buds but will have your friends clawing for more. These frostings will pile atop your cupcakes, drip over the edges of your cakes, fill your whoopie pies, top your salads (no, I'm not kidding), and make you feel like you can conquer the highest, sweetest mountaintops! What are you waiting for? Let's take a look at some classics!

Vanilla Buttercream

YIELD: FROSTS ABOUT 1½ DOZEN CUPCAKES

Vanilla Buttercream was the first frosting I learned how to make—and the most difficult. Honestly, I put a lot of pressure on myself to make sure this frosting was perfect since it would become the basis of so many other frostings. Fortunately, my Vanilla Buttercream now tastes fantastical and dreamy, like rainbows and unicorns. Whip this perfect amount of powdery sugar and soft butter into creamy, fluffy peaks; take a sweet taste; and you'll be transported to the heavens. You've never tried anything like it—guaranteed!

1 cup unsalted butter, softened
1 tablespoon pure vanilla extract
3 cups 10x powdered sugar
⅛ teaspoon salt

Mix butter at room temperature in a stand mixer with the paddle attachment until soft, about 3 minutes. Add vanilla and continue mixing about 1 minute. Slowly add powdered sugar and continue mixing after each incorporation of sugar, until all the sugar is in the bowl. Add salt and continue mixing until light and fluffy, about 5 minutes. Scrape sides and bottom of bowl to ensure all ingredients are fully incorporated and distributed evenly.

Extra Sweets!

Other frosting uses: Vanilla Cupcakes (see recipe), as a cookie cake frosting, or whoopie pie filling.

Vanilla Cupcakes
with Vanilla Buttercream

Vanilla Cupcakes

YIELD: MAKES ABOUT 1–2 DOZEN

2½ cups all-purpose flour
1 teaspoon baking powder
½ teaspoon baking soda
½ teaspoon salt
3 eggs
2 cups sugar
1 cup canola oil
2 teaspoons pure vanilla extract
1 cup sour cream
1 batch Vanilla Buttercream

1. Preheat oven to 325°F. Sift flour, baking powder, baking soda, and salt into a bowl.

2. In a separate mixing bowl on low speed, beat the eggs and sugar until thick; scrape the sides and bottom of the bowl when done. Add in oil and vanilla until well blended. Mix in the sour cream. Add dry ingredient mixture and blend until smooth.

3. Scoop into cupcake pans and bake for 10–12 minutes. Test the cupcakes with a toothpick, and when done remove from oven and transfer to a cooling rack to cool. Frost with the Vanilla Buttercream by spreading with a knife or piping with a bag.

Chocolate Buttercream

YIELD: FROSTS ABOUT 2½ DOZEN CUPCAKES

When I was ten years old my mom would run off to Jazzercise each Saturday morning in her neon leotard, stopping at the donut shop on her way home for plate-sized half-moon cookies. These were soft, moist, inch-thick chocolate cookies, half covered in a fudgy dense chocolate buttercream and the other half drenched in a pure white vanilla buttercream. This Chocolate Buttercream frosting is my attempt at recreating the chocolate part of those delicious half-moon cookies that I swear my mom bought to stoke my frosting obsession at an early age.

2 cups unsalted butter, softened
1 tablespoon plus 1 teaspoon pure vanilla extract
⅔ cup unsweetened cocoa powder
½ teaspoon salt
5 cups powdered sugar
¾ of a 16-ounce jar of your favorite fudge (I love Mrs. Richardson's)

Cream butter until smooth by placing it in the mixing bowl fitted with the paddle attachment and mix on low speed, about 2 minutes. Add vanilla and continue mixing an additional minute. Sift cocoa powder and add to mixture. Sift salt with sugar and add to bowl slowly and continue mixing about 3 minutes. Mix in fudge and whip until fluffy, about 5 minutes.

Extra Sweets!

Other frosting uses: Chocolate Cupcakes (see recipe), frost brownies, or spread on graham crackers with marshmallows to create s'mores.

Chocolate Cupcakes with
Chocolate Buttercream

Chocolate Cupcakes

YIELD: MAKES ABOUT 18 CUPCAKES

¾ cup unsweetened cocoa powder

1½ cups flour

1½ cups sugar

1½ teaspoons baking soda

¾ teaspoon baking powder

¾ teaspoon salt

2 large eggs

¾ cup warm water

¾ cup buttermilk

4 tablespoons applesauce

1½ teaspoons pure vanilla extract

1 batch Chocolate Buttercream

1. Preheat oven to 325°F. Sift all dry ingredients together in large bowl. Add all wet ingredients except frosting and mix well.

2. Scoop into lined cupcake pans and bake 10–12 minutes or until toothpick inserted in center comes out with cake on it, not batter. Remove from oven and allow to cool. Frost with Chocolate Buttercream.

CREAM CHEESE FROSTING

YIELD: FROSTS ABOUT 1½ DOZEN CUPCAKES

Cream cheese frosting is what makes carrot cake more than just vegetable bread and red velvet cupcakes more than just dyed chocolate cake. How could these cakes not inspire me to create my own version of something so amazing! The tang of the cream cheese mixed with the sweetness of the powdered sugar makes this frosting so balanced yet incredibly unique. Try to serve red velvet cupcakes without cream cheese frosting and you'll have a riot on your hands. Heck, save yourself a step and just serve this Cream Cheese Frosting on its own! I swear no one will even ask for cake once they taste this creamy deliciousness.

¼ cup unsalted butter
8 ounces cream cheese
1½ teaspoons pure vanilla extract
2 cups powdered sugar

Cream butter by placing it in the mixing bowl fitted with the paddle attachment and mix on low speed, about 2 minutes until smooth. Add cream cheese and mix well about 3 minutes, until smooth. Mix in vanilla and powdered sugar and beat until well blended and no lumps.

Extra Sweets!

Other frosting uses: Red Velvet Cupcakes (see recipe), carrot cake frosting, or as a bagel spread with craisins on top.

Red Velvet Cupcakes with
Cream Cheese Frosting

Red Velvet Cupcakes

YIELD: ABOUT 1 DOZEN CUPCAKES

¼ cup butter
¾ cup white sugar
1 egg
½ cup buttermilk
½ teaspoon pure vanilla extract
1 tablespoon red food coloring
¾ teaspoon baking soda
1½ teaspoons distilled white vinegar
1 cup flour
2 tablespoons plus 2 teaspoons unsweetened cocoa powder
½ teaspoon salt
½ cup applesauce
1 batch Cream Cheese Frosting

1. Preheat oven to 350°F. Cream butter by placing it in the mixing bowl fitted with the paddle attachment and mix on low speed, about 2 minutes until smooth, then add sugar slowly and cream together until fluffy, about 2 minutes. Mix in eggs, buttermilk, vanilla, and red food coloring. Add applesauce and mix another 20 seconds.

2. In a separate small bowl, mix baking soda and vinegar. It will fizzle, and when it stops fizzling, mix into batter.

3. Combine flour, cocoa powder, and salt, and mix into batter. Scoop into cupcake tins and bake until toothpick inserted comes out clean, about 10–12 minutes. Remove from oven and allow to cool. Once cool, frost generously with Cream Cheese Frosting.

Strawberry Frosting

When I first started selling cupcakes, I realized that I needed more than three frosting recipes to start a business! Fortunately, my Vanilla Buttercream is so versatile that just by adding a bit of chopped fresh fruit or crushed cookie and whipping it like mad you'll have a whole new magical flavor on your hands. I first transformed my Vanilla Buttercream into this Strawberry Frosting, which has the same flavor that you'll find in Neapolitan ice cream (my Dad's favorite), but with fresh juicy strawberries bursting through each bite. Delicious!

1 cup unsalted butter, softened
1 tablespoon pure vanilla extract
3 cups 10x powdered sugar
⅛ teaspoon salt
4 fresh small strawberries, diced (If your strawberries are larger, add less. If you add too many strawberries, the juice will cause the frosting to congeal, so be careful.)

In the bowl of a stand mixer fitted with the paddle attachment, beat butter until creamy, about 2 minutes. Add vanilla and continue mixing an additional minute. Add sugar and salt slowly, and beat until light and fluffy, about 3 minutes. Add diced strawberries and continue mixing until mixture is light, pink, and fluffy.

Extra Sweets!

Other frosting uses: Strawberry-Frosted Limoncello "Shortcakes" (see recipe), fresh pineapple dip, or spread on banana chips.

Strawberry-Frosted Limoncello
"Shortcakes" with Strawberry Frosting

Strawberry-Frosted Limoncello "Shortcakes"

YIELD: MAKES 6 SHORTCAKES

1 roll buttermilk biscuits
1 ounce limoncello
½ batch Strawberry Frosting
6 fresh strawberries

1. Bake biscuits according to package directions. Remove from oven and slice each in half. Lightly soak the bottom halves of the biscuits with limoncello by slowly pouring limoncello over the inside with a teaspoon.

2. Fill a Ziploc bag or a pastry bag with Strawberry Frosting. Dollop frosting on the limoncello-soaked half of the biscuit, then cover with remaining half of the biscuit.

3. Lightly soak top half of biscuit with limoncello by again slowly pouring limoncello over it with a teaspoon; it will soak into the biscuit. Dollop Strawberry Frosting on top, and adorn each with a strawberry.

Salted Caramel Frosting

YIELD: FROSTS 2 DOZEN MINI APPLE TARTS

At some point over the past few years, the hipster scene smacked into the dessert scene, and salted caramel became the trendiest flavor to ever hop on a bicycle with one pant leg rolled up. Salted caramel tarts, salted caramel ice cream, and salted caramel caramels—you can't pick up a dessert menu without coming face to face with a salted caramel listing. I'm not one to hop on bandwagons, but let's face it: Who doesn't love salted caramel? Enter this Salted Caramel Frosting! It's delicious enough to eat on its own, but it really shines when used to top a piping-hot batch of the Salted Caramel Apple Tarts found here.

4 tablespoons unsalted butter
1 cup packed brown sugar
Pinch coarse sea salt

½ cup heavy cream
1 tablespoon pure vanilla extract
½ teaspoon cinnamon

1. In a medium pot over medium heat, cook butter, sugar, salt, and cream, stirring continuously for about 5–7 minutes. Add vanilla and cinnamon and stir over heat another 1–2 minutes until creamy and slightly thick. Don't overcook; it will thicken more as it cools.

2. Remove from heat and pour in a bowl to cool. Use this as a frosting for the apple tarts or add 2–4 tablespoons of it to Vanilla Buttercream (see recipe in this part) for a whipped, fluffy caramel buttercream. Note: The caramel will harden when stored; heat in microwave for 10–20 seconds to loosen up if you're going to use it later.

Extra Sweets!

Other frosting uses: Salted Caramel Apple Tarts (see recipe), pretzel dip, ice cream topping, or add 2–4 tablespoons of it to Vanilla Buttercream frosting (see recipe in this part) for a whipped, fluffy caramel buttercream.

Salted Caramel Apple Tarts
with Salted Caramel Frosting

Salted Caramel Apple Tarts

YIELD: 1 DOZEN TARTS

1 Honeycrisp apple, chopped
1 batch Salted Caramel Frosting, divided
1 teaspoon cinnamon, plus ½ teaspoon more for sprinkling
1 dozen (store-bought) phyllo cups

1. Cook the chopped apple in a medium saucepot over low heat. Add 3 tablespoons Salted Caramel Frosting and 1 teaspoon cinnamon, and stir until the apples are tender, about 10–15 minutes.

2. Remove from heat, scoop into phyllo cups, sprinkle with cinnamon, and drizzle remaining Salted Caramel Frosting on top.

MINT CHOCOLATE CHIP FROSTING

YIELD: FROSTS 1 TRIFLE DISH

Know what's better than mint chocolate chip ice cream? This Mint Chocolate Chip Frosting. It's creamy, doesn't drip down your hands, and tastes just as great in a snowstorm as it does at the beach. I like to throw on my man-sized sweatshirt and fuzzy slippers, and curl up with a snack loaded with Mint Chocolate Chip Frosting. You don't want to do that with your mint chocolate chip ice cream, do you? Just one more reason to fall in love with this Mint Chocolate Chip Frosting!

1½ cups butter
1½ tablespoons pure vanilla extract
3¼ cups powdered sugar
Pinch of salt
6 drops green food coloring
1 cup Andes Crème de Menthe Thins candies, chopped

In the bowl of a stand mixer fitted with the paddle attachment, beat butter until creamy by mixing on low speed, about 2 minutes, until smooth. Add vanilla and continue mixing another minute. Slowly add sugar and salt and beat until light and fluffy, about 3 minutes. Add the chopped Andes candies and green food coloring, and whip for another 2–3 minutes until creamy and an even color.

Extra Sweets!

Other frosting uses: Mint Chocolate Cookie Trifle (see recipe), topping chocolate cupcakes with a peppermint patty baked inside, or sandwiched between two Thin Mints cookies.

Mint Chocolate Cookie
Trifle with Mint Chocolate
Chip Frosting

Mint Chocolate Cookie Trifle

YIELD: 6–8 INDIVIDUAL TRIFLES

1 cup unsalted butter, softened
1 teaspoon pure vanilla extract
3 cups flour
½ teaspoon baking powder
¾ teaspoon salt
⅔ cup cocoa powder
1 cup applesauce
1 batch Mint Chocolate Chip Frosting, divided
3 tablespoons Baileys Irish Cream (optional)
6–8 Andes Mint Chocolate Candy candies, chopped

1. Preheat oven to 350°F. In the bowl of a stand mixer fitted with paddle attachment, whip butter by placing on low speed, about 2 minutes until smooth, then add vanilla and mix to combine.

2. In a separate bowl, mix flour, baking powder, salt, and cocoa. Add flour mixture to butter mixture and continue mixing about 1 minute. Add applesauce and continue mixing until all ingredients are well incorporated.

3. Spread half the cookie dough in an 8" × 8" brownie pan. Spread a very thin layer of frosting on top. Spread the remainder of cookie dough on top. Bake for 18–20 minutes or until a toothpick inserted into the center comes out clean. Remove from oven and cool.

4. Press 3 tablespoons cookie into the bottom of individual trifle dishes. Drizzle lightly with Baileys (if you're going for the adult version). Spread a layer of Mint Chocolate Chip Frosting on top, and then alternate layering the cookie, Baileys, and frosting until you reach the top. Garnish with chopped Andes candies.

 Peanut Butter Buttercream

YIELD: FROSTS ABOUT 1½ DOZEN CUPCAKES

My basic resume of frostings would not be complete without my amazing Peanut Butter Buttercream. It's so amazing, in fact, that I pulled it out of my frosting repertoire as my secret weapon to win the second round on Cupcake Wars! *Knowing that this frosting was guaranteed to win over the judges, I built the Ultimate Dude Peanut Butter Cookie Dough Cupcake around it, with the focus on the sweet pile of Peanut Butter Buttercream on top. If there was one thing I was 100 percent confident about that day, it was that the judges would* love *this frosting. And love it they did!*

1 cup unsalted butter, softened
1½ cups creamy peanut butter (my go-to brand has always been Peter Pan)
2 teaspoons pure vanilla extract
3¼ cups powdered sugar

Cream butter by placing it in the mixing bowl fitted with the paddle attachment and mix on low speed, about 2 minutes until smooth. Add in peanut butter and beat until smooth, about 3 minutes. Add vanilla and continue mixing an additional minute. Add sugar and mix until light and fluffy, about 5 minutes.

Extra Sweets

Other frosting uses: Ultimate Dude Peanut Butter Cookie Dough Cupcakes (see recipe), spread on bacon slices, melted over ice cream, or just scooped up with your fingers.

Ultimate Dude Peanut Butter Cookie Dough Cupcakes with Peanut Butter Buttercream

Ultimate Dude Peanut Butter Cookie Dough Cupcakes

COOKIE DOUGH FILLING

YIELD: APPROXIMATELY 3 CUPS
. . . .

2¼ cups all-purpose flour
1 teaspoon baking soda
1 teaspoon salt
1 cup butter, softened
¾ cups granulated sugar
¾ cups light brown sugar, packed
1 teaspoon pure vanilla extract
¼ cup milk
12 ounces semisweet chocolate chips

For Cookie Dough Filling: Combine flour, baking soda, and salt in a small bowl and set aside. In the bowl of an electric stand mixer using a paddle attachment, beat butter, granulated sugar, brown sugar, and vanilla extract until creamy, about 3 minutes. Add milk and mix an additional 2 minutes. Gradually, on low speed and in several additions, beat in flour mixture. Stir in chocolate chips by hand until well combined. Divide in half and set one half in cooler to chill. Reserve the other half for the Fondant-Covered Chocolate Chip Cookie Tires.

Fondant-Covered Chocolate Chip Cookie Tires

YIELD: 2–3 DOZEN TIRES

½ batch Cookie Dough Filling
Black fondant, rolled (you can buy this at any baking store)
24–36 white chocolate candy melts

For Fondant-Covered Chocolate Chip Cookie Tires: Preheat oven to 375°F. Take the cookie dough that you set aside and roll out on a parchment-lined baking sheet to ¼-inch thickness. Bake for 9–11 minutes or until golden brown. Remove from oven and allow to cool. Cut out circles of cookies with a circular cookie cutter. Roll out fondant and cut out circles of fondant with a circular cookie cutter slightly larger than the cutter you used for the cookies. Wrap the fondant circle around the cookie circle. Stick one white chocolate candy melt in the center of the fondant-covered cookie so that it sticks. Using the V point of a star-shaped cookie cutter, press "tire treads" all around the sides of the fondant-covered cookie.

For Assembly

Chocolate Cupcakes (see recipe in this part)
½ batch Cookie Dough Filling
Peanut Butter Buttercream
¼ cup Salted Caramel Frosting (see recipe in this part)
1 tablespoon kosher salt
Fondant-Covered Chocolate Chip Cookie Tires (optional)

To assemble Ultimate Dude Peanut Butter Cookie Dough Cupcakes: Cut a hole in the center of a chocolate cupcake with a paring knife and scoop ½ tablespoon of Cookie Dough Filling into the center. Replace the piece of cake you cut out. Generously frost the top of the cupcake with the Peanut Butter Buttercream. Drizzle with Salted Caramel Frosting and sprinkle with kosher salt. Place the Fondant-Covered Chocolate Chip Cookie Tire on top if desired.

Lemon Glaze Frosting

YIELD: ½ CUP FROSTING TO FROST 3 CUPS FROSTING FRUIT SALAD

When life hands you lemons, make lemon frosting! Squeezing fresh lemons into a bowl of powdered sugar really does have the ability to replace sadness with sweetness in sour situations. Even when I'm feeling down, I find time to hit the nearest grocery store, purchase the shiniest and brightest lemons I can find, then squeeze the living juice out of them. Did you know that lemons are like little stress balls? If you put your frustration into this recipe, you'll find that sour has a tendency to bring about the sweet.

¾ cup powdered sugar
3 tablespoons lemon juice
Zest of 1 lemon

Place all ingredients in a bowl and whisk until smooth. Easiest frosting ever!

Extra Sweets

Other frosting uses: Frosting Fruit Salad (see recipe), poured over a sliced grapefruit, or used to glaze shortbread cookies.

Frosting Fruit Salad

YIELD: SERVES 4–6

1 pint fresh strawberries
1 pint fresh blueberries
1 pint fresh blackberries
1 pint fresh raspberries
1 lemon, cut into wedges for garnish
1 batch Lemon Glaze Frosting

Quarter strawberries. Place all berries in a bowl, then drizzle with Lemon Glaze Frosting. Toss, garnish with a lemon wedge, and serve!

Frosting Fruit
Salad with Lemon
Glaze Frosting

Cookies and Cream Ice
Cream Trifle with Cookies
and Cream Frosting

COOKIES AND CREAM FROSTING

YIELD: ABOUT 2 CUPS, ENOUGH TO MAKE ONE LARGE TRIFLE OR 6–8 INDIVIDUAL TRIFLES

Remember that time you ate a whole sleeve of Oreos? Yeah, I've repressed that memory, too. Next time you're tempted by that big blue box, take a sleeve and dump them in the food processor instead. The good news is that you can no longer inhale a sleeve of Oreos because they're all crushed up! The better news is that your Oreos are now a base for this fresh and fabulous, homemade Cookies and Cream Frosting! Enjoy!

¾ cup white chocolate chips
¼ cup milk chocolate chips
1 cup heavy cream
1 cup Oreo cookies, cream removed, finely crushed

Combine white and milk chocolate chips in a medium bowl. In a small saucepot over medium heat, boil heavy cream until it starts to foam. Remove from heat and pour over bowl of chips. Whisk until all chocolate is melted. Stir in 1 cup Oreo crumbs. Allow mixture to cool in the fridge until it starts to thicken. Once completely cool, remove from fridge and place in the bowl of a stand mixer fitted with the whisk attachment. Beat on high until light and fluffy, about 5 minutes.

Extra Sweets!

Other frosting uses: Cookies and Cream Ice Cream Trifle (see recipe), fill an Oreo pie crust with frosting and decorate with whipped cream and Oreos, or spread on top of chocolate cheesecake.

Cookies and Cream
Ice Cream Trifle

YIELD: MAKES ABOUT 4–8 ½-CUP SERVINGS

At this point, as you're hovering over your masterpiece of Cookies and Cream Frosting, you should feel a rush of pride in what you've created along with a sense of strength over that damn sleeve of neatly stacked cookies. Now the world is your oyster with this frosting, but just like in those Choose Your Own Adventure *books from the 1990s, I'm going to let you stop here and choose your own cookies & dream path . . .*

OPTION A

Are you going to a party? Having friends over? Attending a family dinner? Thanking your neighbor for something? If you answered yes to any of these, you'll need:

Giant trifle bowl
1 batch Cookies and Cream Frosting
2 cups chocolate ice cream
2 cups vanilla ice cream
2 tablespoons Oreo cookies, finely crushed

For the A people: Take a giant spoon and cover the bottom of the trifle bowl with your Cookies and Cream Frosting to about ½" thickness. Then take 1 cup of the chocolate ice cream and spread it on top of the frosting to about ½" thickness. This works best if you let the ice cream warm up a bit before spreading it. Repeat once again with the vanilla ice cream to about ½" thickness. Repeat the layering again with the frosting, chocolate ice cream, and vanilla ice cream, until you've reached the top of the dish. Sprinkle some Oreo crumbs on top for decoration, cover the dish, and toss it back in the freezer until you're ready to serve.

OPTION B

Are you gloriously on your own? No shame in this—I'm always the B girl. In this case you'll need:

Mini airtight containers
½ batch Cookies and Cream Frosting
1 cup chocolate ice cream
1 cup vanilla ice cream
2 tablespoons Oreo cookies, finely crushed

For the B people: Follow the same directions as the A people, just on a smaller scale, in smaller dishes. Pack your mini Cookies and Cream Ice Cream Trifles in the freezer for the next time your Oreo craving strikes, and I promise you won't even be tempted by that sleeve.

PEPPERMINT BUTTERCREAM

YIELD: 2 CUPS FROSTING

Peppermint is cool. It's calming. It's smooth, serene, and swirled with existential peace. In other words, peppermint is not me. Let's be honest, though. After just one taste of this creamy Peppermint Buttercream, my spazziness actually slowed for a second—just one second, but it still counts! In this recipe, the crunchiness of the peppermint candies adds a surprising texture to the creaminess of the buttercream, and the red candy color mixes with the white, transforming the frosting into pearly, pastel pink perfection. It's just the thing to savor at the end of a long day—or anytime at all, really!

1 cup unsalted butter, softened
1 tablespoon pure vanilla extract
Pinch of salt
2½ cups powdered sugar
20 hard peppermint candies, finely crushed

In the bowl of a stand mixer with a paddle attachment, cream butter until soft, about 3 minutes on medium speed. Add vanilla, salt, and sugar and continue mixing. Add crushed peppermint candies to bowl and continue mixing until peppermints are well incorporated and frosting is thick and creamy, about 5 minutes.

Extra Sweets!

Other frosting uses: Peppermint Cookie Cups with Peppermint Ice Cream (see recipe), as a dip for peppermint bark, or add 2 tablespoons to a vanilla milkshake and blend.

Peppermint Cookie Cups
with Peppermint Ice Cream

YIELD: MAKES 4–6 COOKIE CUPS

5 tablespoons plus 1 cup Peppermint Buttercream
30 vanilla wafer cookies, crushed; reserve any leftover crumbs for garnish
3 cups vanilla ice cream

1. Preheat oven to 350°F. In a medium bowl, mix 5 tablespoons Peppermint Buttercream with crushed vanilla wafer cookies until the cookies begin to stick together, like a pie crust. Press 2 tablespoons of cookie mixture into each cup of a cupcake tin. Bake in oven about 10 minutes, until they just start to brown. Let cool and place in freezer, in pan, until you're ready to fill with the ice cream.

2. In a medium bowl with a wooden spatula, mix 3 cups slightly softened vanilla ice cream with 1 cup Peppermint Buttercream. Mix until the frosting is evenly swirled throughout the ice cream, until your arm hurts, or until you really just want to eat it. Place bowl in the freezer for about 5–10 minutes to firm the ice cream up again.

3. Remove cookie cups and ice cream from freezer and carefully remove cookie cups from the tin. Scoop 2 or 3 scoops of ice cream in each cookie cup with an ice cream scoop. Sprinkle leftover cookie crumbs on top. Note: These also make great late-night snacks if you store the cookie cups in the freezer in an airtight container and the ice cream in the freezer in a separate airtight container, then scoop as you see fit!

Peppermint Cookie Cups
with Peppermint Ice Cream
and Peppermint Buttercream

Mocha Upside-Down Cupcakes
with Mocha Frosting

Mocha Frosting

YIELD: FILLS AND FROSTS ABOUT 1 DOZEN UPSIDE-DOWN CUPCAKES

While working at numerous coffee shops in the past, I've learned that even noncoffee drinkers partake in the rich delight of a mocha latte now and then. Although I refuse to add chocolate to my coffee, you best believe that I'm A-Okay with adding coffee to my chocolate. Just a hint of your favorite espresso will liven up this fudgy Mocha Frosting like you wouldn't believe, and the rich aromas of freshly brewed espresso will awaken you just enough to tide you over until this frosting is finished whipping . . . if you can wait that long to dig in!

½ cup unsalted butter, softened
1 cup powdered sugar
Pinch of salt
1 tablespoon cocoa powder
1½ teaspoons espresso

In the bowl of a stand mixer fitted with the paddle attachment, mix butter until smooth, about 3 minutes. Add sugar, salt, and cocoa and continue mixing, about 3 minutes. Add espresso to bowl and mix 3–5 minutes, until light and fluffy.

Extra Sweets!

Other frosting uses: Mocha Upside-Down Cupcakes (see recipe), frost cake donuts and serve with coffee, or scoop a tablespoon over espresso sorbet.

Mocha Upside-Down Cupcakes

YIELD: MAKES ABOUT 1 DOZEN CUPCAKES

½ cup olive oil
3 eggs
1½ cups white sugar
3 teaspoons instant espresso, or brewed espresso
1½ teaspoons salt
1½ teaspoons baking powder
½ cup melted milk chocolate
½ cup melted dark chocolate
½ cup buttermilk
1¾ cups plus 2 tablespoons flour
1 batch Mocha Frosting
1 tablespoon cocoa powder for garnish (optional)

1. Preheat oven to 350°F. In the bowl of a stand mixer fitted with a paddle attachment, mix olive oil, eggs, sugar, espresso, salt, and baking powder. Mix milk and dark chocolates and add to the bowl, making sure the chocolate mixture is not hot, just warm. Add buttermilk and mix to incorporate all ingredients. Add flour and mix until just blended, about 30 seconds.

2. Spray a cupcake tin with nonstick cooking spray. Fill tins ¾ full of batter and bake 20–25 minutes, or until a toothpick inserted in the center comes out clean. Remove from oven and allow to cool.

3. Carefully use a butter knife to release edges of cupcakes from the tin and pop each cupcake out. Flip the cupcakes upside down and cut a nickel-sized hole in the center of the bottom all the way through each one. Fill with Mocha Frosting, adding an extra dollop on top. Sprinkle with cocoa powder (if using), say a little prayer thanking the cupcake gods for this amazing upside-down concoction, and devour.

RASPBERRY BUTTERCREAM

YIELD: MAKES ABOUT 1½ CUPS

You can't eat frosting all day without adding something green into the mix—and the Andes candies in the Mint Chocolate Chip Frosting (see recipe in this part) don't count. Inspired by salad, this fruity Raspberry Buttercream revolutionized spinach for me—and hopefully it will do the same for you! Did you ever think of raspberry vinaigrette as essentially being just a runny frosting for salad? Neither did I until I made this Raspberry Buttercream with freshly crushed raspberries and dolloped it on spinach leaves with cocoa-roasted almonds. Mind blown.

½ cup unsalted butter, softened
1¼ cups 10x powdered sugar
½ tablespoon pure vanilla extract
Small pinch of salt
2 or 3 fresh raspberries

In the bowl of a stand mixer, whip butter by placing it in the mixing bowl fitted with the paddle attachment and mix on low speed, about 2 minutes until smooth. Add sugar, vanilla, salt, and raspberries and continue whipping until fluffy, about 5 minutes.

Extra Sweets!

Other frosting uses: Spinach "Salad" (see recipe), as the filling in thumbprint cookies, or mix ½ tablespoon into your plain yogurt.

Spinach "Salad" with
Raspberry Buttercream

Spinach "Salad"

YIELD: ABOUT 24 SPINACH "SALAD SPOONS"

2 tablespoons cocoa powder
1 teaspoon white sugar
1 tablespoon water
⅔ cup raw almonds
1 bag fresh spinach
½ cup Raspberry Buttercream

1. Preheat oven to 350°F. Combine cocoa powder, sugar, water, and almonds in a large Zip-loc bag; seal and shake until almonds are evenly coated in sugar, cocoa, and water. The water will help the sugar and cocoa stick to the almonds. Remove almonds from bag and place on nonstick baking sheet. Place in the oven and bake for about 8–10 minutes.

2. To assemble the "salad," place spinach leaves on a platter, curved side up so that they sit like mini spoons. The amount of spinach spoons you get out of 1 bag of spinach will depend on the quality of the spinach. If I'm serving to guests, I like to use only the perfectly shaped leaves. If I'm alone, I'll use the whole bag. Place about ½ teaspoon of Raspberry Buttercream on each spinach leaf (use the almonds to scoop if you want), then top with almonds. The frosting is the glue that holds the almond to the leaf. Serve!

S'MORE FROSTING

YIELD: FILLS ABOUT 2 DOZEN PUSH-POPS

My first attempt at my cupcake shop didn't go so well, and when I realized that I had to start the cupcake business over again from scratch, I balled my eyes out. When life as you know it crumbles to pieces, I firmly believe that you're allowed to throw that tantrum—grade-school style, flailing limbs and all. But then you'd better pick yourself up and push yourself upwards, because there is s'more work to be done (and because no one looks good eating frosting with a frown). Enter this amazing S'more Frosting! Guaranteed to brighten even the worst day!

4 egg whites
1½ cups white sugar
⅛ teaspoon salt
1 teaspoon cream of tartar
1½ teaspoons pure vanilla extract
4 tablespoons chocolate fudge
6 sheets graham crackers, ground

In a double boiler over medium heat, mix egg whites, sugar, salt, and cream of tartar, and whisk continuously for about 5–6 minutes. Once it becomes frothy and white, remove from heat and immediately pour in stand mixer fitted with whisk attachment. Whisk for 6–9 minutes on high. Add vanilla, fudge, and ground graham crackers; mix slowly for another 1–2 minutes or until well combined.

Extra Sweets!

Other frosting uses: S'more Push-Pop Parfaits (see recipe); in a bowl, sprinkled with graham crackers; or as a fondue dip.

S'more Push-Pop Parfaits
with S'more Frosting

S'more Push-Pop Parfaits

YIELD: MAKES ABOUT 20

½ cup ground graham crackers with extra for garnish, plus 1 sheet for
　　pieces for the bottom of the push-pops
1 package chocolate instant pudding prepared according to package
1 batch S'more Frosting

1. Place a small piece of graham cracker in the bottom of each push-pop or parfait dish. Immediately scoop a spoonful of pudding over the graham cracker piece before the pudding sets.

2. Scoop or pipe a layer of frosting, then sprinkle a layer of crushed graham crackers, and add another layer of pudding, exchanging each layer until you reach the top. Garnish with a pinch of sprinkled crushed graham crackers. If using push-pops, stop before you reach the top so that you can place the lid on. Refrigerate about 15 minutes to set.

PART 2

With ~ A TWIST

Life doesn't always go the way you imagine it will, but luckily for us frosting lovers, we have ways to sweeten the course! Did you rip a hole in your new jacket or get caught tweeting about your boss? Rush home and whip up some Toffee Honey Frosting and chill for the evening! You've earned it. Are the kids complaining about how you never let them eat the raw cookie dough because the eggs might make them sick? Make a batch of eggless Cookie Dough Frosting and let them dig in; you might win mom of the year for this one! The truth is, life isn't perfect, but the frostings that you'll find in this part are unique, delicious, and inspired twists on favorites that just make everything better! So go whip up some Bananas Foster Frosting, tweet some pics to your "friends," and we'll do the secret happy frosting dance to celebrate (my mom taught me this one)!

BROWN SUGAR FROSTING

YIELD: FROSTS 1–2 DOZEN CUPCAKES

In round two on Cupcake Wars, we had one hour to create, bake, decorate, and plate three unique cupcakes for the Monster Jam Pit Party that would be judged 50 percent on taste and 50 percent on decoration. This Brown Sugar Frosting helped us on both counts! This is a cooked frosting, which means it needs to be cooled before it's applied to the cupcake. This just added to the difficulty level of the challenge, but it was worth it! The judges loved *this recipe, and I moved on to the final round. No matter how you look at it, this frosting is a winner!*

½ cup unsalted butter
1 cup light brown sugar, packed
¼ cup milk
2 cups confectioners' sugar, sifted

In a saucepan, melt ½ cup butter. Add the brown sugar and bring to a boil over medium heat for 2 minutes, stirring constantly. Add the milk and bring to a boil, stirring constantly. Remove from heat and allow to cool in freezer to lukewarm. Gradually add the confectioners' sugar and beat with a mixer about 5–7 minutes until thick. If frosting is too thick or crumbly, add small amounts of milk until it is smooth.

Extra Sweets!

Other frosting uses: Sweet Potato Fries and Blueberry Ketchup Cupcakes (see recipe), spread over mashed sweet potatoes, or layer between spice cake.

Sweet Potato Fries and
Blueberry Ketchup Cupcakes
with Brown Sugar Frosting

Sweet Potato Fries and Blueberry Ketchup Cupcakes

YIELD: 1½ DOZEN CUPCAKES AND APPROXIMATELY 2 CUPS BLUEBERRY KETCHUP FILLING

FOR CAKE

2 cups all-purpose flour
2 teaspoons baking powder
½ teaspoon baking soda
¼ teaspoon salt
1 teaspoon cinnamon, ground
½ teaspoon nutmeg
½ teaspoon chili powder
1 cup unsalted butter, softened
1½ cups sugar
3 large eggs
17 ounces sweet potato purée
½ teaspoon vanilla extract

1. Preheat the oven to 300°F. Line 2 cupcake or muffin pans with 18 cupcake liners. Sift the flour, baking powder, baking soda, salt, cinnamon, nutmeg, and chili powder into a medium-size bowl and set aside. In the bowl of an electric stand mixer with a paddle attachment, cream the butter and sugar together until light and fluffy, about 2 minutes starting on low speed and then switching to medium speed. Beat in the eggs one at a time on low, scraping down the bowl after each addition. Mix in the sweet potatoes and vanilla extract, beating just until combined. Add the dry ingredients slowly on low, mixing just until incorporated, about 1–2 minutes.

2. Fill 18 cupcake liners ¾ full and bake for 18 minutes or until a toothpick inserted in the center comes out clean. Cool the cupcakes completely.

For Blueberry Ketchup Filling

2 cups blueberries
2 tablespoons apple cider vinegar
4 tablespoons light brown sugar, packed
½ teaspoon dry ginger
¼ teaspoon salt

For Assembly

1 batch Brown Sugar Frosting

3. Combine all the filling ingredients in a heavy saucepan and bring to a boil over medium heat, stirring frequently and mashing the blueberries with a fork. Let simmer, about 10 minutes. Remove from heat and place in the refrigerator until completely cool.

4. Cut a small hole in the center of each cupcake and scoop 1 teaspoon of Blueberry Ketchup Filling inside. Place the cake that you removed from the hole back on top, pressing down lightly. Put the Brown Sugar Frosting into a pastry bag and cut ½" off the tip. While squeezing the bag, swirl a dollop on top of each cupcake. This frosting will harden when it's cold, so make sure it's at room temperature before you frost.

Chocolate Chip Cookie Wafers
with Cookie Dough Frosting

Cookie Dough Frosting

YIELD: FROSTS 8–10 CHOCOLATE CHIP COOKIE WAFERS

Cookie dough frosting—because who doesn't like cookie dough? And, in fact, this Cookie Dough Frosting is so much more than frosting; it's actual spreadable, bakeable cookie dough. And since it's eggless, you can feel completely safe eating it in its raw form! Eat it with a spoon, eat it with your fingers, or bake it in the oven and then spread it back on top as the frosting on your warm, crispy cookie wafers. You can't screw this up; I promise.

1 cup unsalted butter, softened
¼ cup granulated sugar
½ cup brown sugar
1 teaspoon salt
1 teaspoon pure vanilla extract
1⅛ cups flour
1 teaspoon baking soda
½ cup semisweet chocolate chips

In the bowl of a stand mixer fitted with a paddle attachment, cream butter until soft by mixing on low speed, about 2 minutes until smooth. Add both sugars, salt, vanilla, flour, baking soda, and chocolate chips and mix until light and fluffy, about 5 minutes.

Extra Sweets!

Other frosting uses: Chocolate Chip Cookie Wafers (see recipe), mixed into ice cream; rolled in a log, then wrapped and given as a gift!

Chocolate Chip Cookie Wafers

YIELD: MAKES ABOUT 8–10 WAFERS

1 batch Cookie Dough Frosting

1. Preheat oven to 350°F. Take half of the frosting and make 1 tablespoon–sized balls on a parchment-lined baking sheet. Bake for 10–12 minutes, until they start to brown. They will spread out and become very flat and wafer like.

2. Remove from oven and cool completely. These are very thin wafer cookies, so be gentle when handling them. Spread remaining Cookie Dough Frosting on top once cool.

TOFFEE HONEY FROSTING

YIELD: ¾ CUP FROSTING

Some of my favorite evenings consist of bursting through my apartment door, tearing off my jeans, throwing on sweats, and jumping on my window seat with my laptop, a glass of malbec, and a frosted snack. I'm a huge fan of Cracker Jacks, but I don't like buying a bag when I can just make my own, even more delicious, frosting-covered popcorn at home! Enter Toffee Honey Frosting! It is finger-lickin' sticky sweet, and this recipe makes just enough for a solo snack, plus leftovers for tomorrow. This frosting doesn't come with a temporary tattoo or a cheap puzzle; instead, the prize is your delight in solitude, which you may have forgotten was possible.

½ cup unsalted butter
½ cup unsweetened condensed milk
2 tablespoons honey
1 tablespoon toffee bits

In a small saucepan over medium heat, stir all ingredients continuously until mixture starts to thicken, boil, and become *slightly* sticky. It will be bubbly and thick, but remove from heat before it browns. Scrape into mixing bowl and whisk for about 5 minutes.

Extra Sweets!

Other frosting uses: Frosted Popcorn (see recipe); coat mixed nuts, spread on baking sheet, and bake in the oven for 5–10 minutes for a chunky brittle; or pour over popcorn, roll into balls, and put into baggies for popcorn ball gifts.

Frosted Popcorn

1 bag microwave popcorn
½ batch Toffee Honey Frosting
1 handful mixed nuts

1. Pop a bag of your favorite microwave popcorn.

2. Drizzle Toffee Honey Frosting over popcorn in bag, add nuts, and shake, shake, shake! Note: Store leftover frosting in airtight container in fridge and reheat for just 30 seconds the next time your frosting craving strikes.

Frosted Popcorn with
Toffee Honey Frosting

Bananas Foster Frosting

YIELD: FROSTS ABOUT 40 CUPCAKE PANCAKE BITES

One of my go-to karaoke songs is "Banana Pancakes" by the incorrigibly sexy Jack Johnson. When I realized that my singing wouldn't top the charts and win the affections of bargoers, I decided to create this buttery, caramel-spice-y Bananas Foster Frosting instead. I figured that people wouldn't notice their ears were bleeding if I fed them frosting whipped with fresh bananas. Delicious frosting and guilt-free, subpar karaoke? Sounds like a win-win to me!

1 cup unsalted butter, softened
2½ cups powdered sugar
Pinch of salt
¾ teaspoon cinnamon
2 tablespoons caramel, store bought
3 slices fresh banana

In the bowl of a stand mixer fitted with the paddle attachment, cream the butter until soft by mixing on low speed, about 2 minutes. Sift together the powdered sugar, salt, and cinnamon in a separate bowl, then add to the bowl of butter and continue mixing about 3–5 minutes. Add caramel and banana slices, and mix another 1–2 minutes until well incorporated and creamy.

Extra Sweets!

Other frosting uses: Bananas Foster Cupcake-Pancake Bites (see recipe); spread on toast with peanut butter; or spread 2 tablespoons onto a frozen banana and drizzle with chocolate sauce.

Bananas Foster Cupcake–Pancake Bites

YIELD: MAKES ABOUT 20 SANDWICHES

1½ bananas, ripe
¾ cup butter, softened
2 cups white sugar
⅛ cup brown sugar
3 large eggs plus 2 eggs (for egg wash)
2 teaspoons vanilla extract
3 cups flour
1½ teaspoons baking soda

¼ teaspoon salt
1½ cups buttermilk
½ cup milk (for egg wash)
1 batch Bananas Foster Frosting
2 tablespoons caramel, store bought, for garnish
1 teaspoon cinnamon for garnish

1. Preheat oven to 350°F. Mash bananas and set aside. In the bowl of a stand mixer fitted with a paddle attachment, beat butter and both sugars together by mixing on low speed, about 2 minutes. Add eggs and vanilla, and continue mixing for 1 minute. In a separate bowl, mix flour, baking soda, and salt. Add a small bit of the flour mixture to the mixture in the stand mixer, then add a small amount of buttermilk. Alternate until all the flour mixture and buttermilk have been added. Add bananas, caramel, and cinnamon and mix until incorporated, about 1–2 minutes.

2. Scoop into mini cupcake pans with liners, filling only ⅔ of the way, and bake for 8–10 minutes.

3. Remove cupcakes from oven and cool. Peel off liners and slice the tops off the cupcakes. Save the stumps in an airtight container for later use in Banana Split Cake Balls (see recipe in this part).

4. In a small bowl, make an egg wash of 2 eggs and ½ cup milk. Spray a nonstick skillet or cast-iron skillet with cooking spray and heat over medium heat. Brush both sides of cupcake tops with egg wash and put in frying pan over medium heat; flip after each side browns, about 1–2 minutes. Remove from heat and allow to cool slightly before spreading Bananas Foster Frosting on one "pancake," drizzling with caramel and sprinkling with cinnamon, and sandwiching with another "pancake."

Bananas Foster Cupcake-Pancake
Bites with Bananas Foster Frosting

Banana Split Cake Balls
with Chocolate Strawberry
Cream Cheese Frosting

Chocolate Strawberry Cream Cheese Frosting

YIELD: MAKES ABOUT 2 CUPS

Have you ever made chocolate-dipped strawberries for yourself? No? Neither have I. Chocolate-dipped strawberries seem like an affectionate, loving, romantic dessert, and it seems weird to make them just for yourself. Know what isn't weird and tastes just like juicy, chocolate-dipped strawberries? This Chocolate Strawberry Cream Cheese Frosting. The tangy cream cheese whipped with freshly sliced juicy red strawberries and deep cocoa powder is oh-so-delicious! It's like giving yourself a hug, in the most un-weird way of all.

8 ounces cream cheese, softened
¼ cup unsalted butter, softened
2 cups powdered sugar
1 tablespoon cocoa powder
1½ teaspoons vanilla
2 fresh strawberries, sliced

In the bowl of a stand mixer fitted with a paddle attachment, mix cream cheese until smooth, about 2 minutes. Add butter and continue mixing an additional 2 minutes. Sift sugar and cocoa together and slowly add to cream cheese mixture and mix about 4 minutes. Add vanilla and strawberries, and mix about 3 minutes until smooth and creamy.

Extra Sweets!

Other frosting uses: Banana Split Cake Balls (see recipe), cut cones out of the center of large strawberries and pipe frosting inside, or frost a red velvet cake.

Banana Split Cake Balls

YIELD: MAKES ABOUT 12 BALLS

1 batch Bananas Foster Cupcake-Pancake Bites cupcake
    stumps (see recipe in this part)
1 batch Chocolate Strawberry Cream Cheese Frosting
1 or 2 bags pink white chocolate melting wafers
Cocoa powder or cake crumbs for decorating

1. In a large bowl, crush up cupcake stumps with your hands until crumbs form. Add Chocolate Strawberry Cream Cheese Frosting a bit at a time and mix well with your hands until the mixture sticks together. Don't add too much frosting or the balls will be too moist and won't hold their shape. Using a mini ice cream scoop, scoop balls and roll between your hands to smooth out.

2. In a microwave-safe bowl, melt pink chocolate wafers at 30-second intervals, stirring in between until they're completely melted. Don't heat too long or they'll burn.

3. Drop cake balls into the chocolate one at a time with a fork, making sure the chocolate fully covers the ball. Raise the fork up with the ball on it and gently shake the excess chocolate off. Drop ball on wax paper, sprinkle with cake crumbs or cocoa powder, and let harden. Repeat with each ball, adding more melted chocolate to your bowl as you go along. Note: The chocolate-covered cake balls will harden fast, so if you're sprinkling them with cake crumbs or cocoa powder, do so quickly or the crumbs won't adhere.

Pumpkin Spice Cream Cheese Frosting

YIELD: FROSTS ABOUT 12 PIZZAS

Every October the world catches pumpkin fever. Seriously, every October. Pumpkin is the chameleon of vegetables, a celebrated one even. It's what every carrot wishes it truly were. My pumpkin heart, though, is devoted solely to the pureness of this Pumpkin Spice Cream Cheese Frosting using real *canned pumpkin. Yup, no artificial flavorings here. Canned pumpkin is just as real as a whole pumpkin and a lot safer to open. It's also more delicious, and what's better than that?!*

4 ounces cream cheese, softened
2 tablespoons unsalted butter, softened
¾ teaspoons vanilla extract
1 cup powdered sugar, sifted
½ teaspoon cinnamon

⅛ teaspoon nutmeg
⅛ teaspoon ginger
1/16 teaspoon clove
2 tablespoons canned pumpkin

Whip cream cheese until smooth by placing it in the mixing bowl fitted with the paddle attachment and mix on high speed, about 2 minutes. Add butter and vanilla and continue mixing about 2–3 minutes. Add sugar and spices and mix until well blended. Add pumpkin and continue mixing about 2 minutes. Scrape bottom and sides of bowl and mix until frosting is smooth and everything is well incorporated, about 3 minutes.

Extra Sweets!

Other frosting uses: Pumpkin Spice Pizzas (see recipe), fill inside fresh pasta pockets to make pumpkin cream cheese raviolis, or fill the inside of pumpkin muffins.

Pumpkin Spice Pizzas with Pumpkin Spice Cream Cheese Frosting

Pumpkin Spice Pizzas

YIELD: 1 ROLL OF DOUGH MAKES 6 PIZZAS

1 roll store-bought biscuit dough
3 tablespoons canned pumpkin
3 teaspoons cinnamon
3 teaspoons brown sugar
1 batch Pumpkin Spice Cream Cheese Frosting
½ cup walnuts (optional)
½ cup pecans (optional)
½ cup chocolate chips (optional)
½ cup graham crackers (optional)
½ cup toasted pumpkin seeds (optional)

1. Preheat oven according to biscuit directions. Remove 1 roll of biscuits from packaging, separate each biscuit, and flatten onto a parchment-lined baking sheet, as you would pizza dough. Spread 2 teaspoons of canned pumpkin on each biscuit, and sprinkle with a pinch of cinnamon and brown sugar. Bake according to package directions, removing from oven when just slightly brown.

2. Place each biscuit on a plate or cooling rack. Scoop Pumpkin Spice Cream Cheese Frosting into a pastry bag or a sealable bag with the tip cut off, and squeeze frosting over each biscuit in the pattern of your choice. You can use as much or as little frosting for this as you like!

3. Top each pizza as you desire, or if you're having a party, just put out dishes of toppings and let your guests go wild. Use walnuts, pecans, chocolate chips, graham crackers, or toasted pumpkin seeds. Once you get going, pumpkin-carving parties will be a thing of the past, and you'll be having frosting parties instead!

Toffee Ganache Frosting

YIELD: MAKES ABOUT 2 DOZEN TRUFFLES

There are times that I'm totally feeling down: my bank account is looking low, that girl whom I secretly hate but only out of envy is vacationing in Maui with her hunky boyfriend, I lost 3 Twitter followers, and my recent blog comments are at zero! These are the times that I make this beyond easy, creamy, and devilishly decadent Toffee Ganache Frosting. This frosting makes me feel like a superstar again (and might make those Twitter un-followers regret they stopped following me), and it's guaranteed to do the same for you!

1 cup milk chocolate chips
½ cup toffee bits
1 cup heavy cream

In a large bowl, mix the milk chocolate chips and toffee bits. Next, in a saucepan over medium heat, simmer heavy cream until it just begins to boil, then remove cream from heat and slowly pour over chocolate and toffee, whisking continuously until chocolate is fully melted. Chill bowl in freezer until it begins to thicken, about 45 minutes. Once cool, whip mixture in stand mixer fitted with whisk attachment until it fluffs up and becomes lighter in color, about 7–8 minutes.

Extra Sweets!

Other frosting uses: Coffee Toffee Ganache Frosting Truffles (see recipe), as a topping for butterscotch pudding, or as a filling for caramel cupcakes.

Coffee Toffee Ganache Frosting Truffles

YIELD: ABOUT 1½ DOZEN TRUFFLES

1 batch Toffee Ganache Frosting, chilled
1 cup chocolate-covered espresso beans, ground

1. Using a mini ice cream scoop, make chilled Toffee Ganache Frosting into balls and drop on wax paper on a baking dish. Place dish in freezer to firm the balls for about 20–30 minutes.

2. Remove balls from freezer and roll in a bowl of crushed espresso beans. Place on a wax-paper–lined dish and return to freezer to set, about 15 minutes.

Vanilla Hazelnut Coffee
Pudding with Hazelnut
Coffee Frosting

Coffee Toffee Ganache
Frosting Truffles

HAZELNUT COFFEE FROSTING

YIELD: ABOUT 2 CUPS

If you meet me someday, there's a very good chance I'll smell like hazelnut coffee. Why? Because I'm a spiller. Almost every morning I spill coffee right down my shirt. It's as though I can't quite gauge the ratio of distance between the cup and my mouth, even after all these years. The fact that you can smell like wonderfully sweet hazelnut coffee without the stains of being a spiller is part of what's so great about this frosting; that and the fact that it's addictively delicious! Genius, right? You can thank me later.

1 cup unsalted butter, softened
1 cup hazelnuts, finely chopped
1 single-serve instant coffee packet
1 tablespoon hot water
2 cups powdered sugar
¼ teaspoon salt
2 teaspoons pure vanilla extract

In the bowl of a stand mixer, cream butter until smooth, about 3 minutes. Add hazelnuts and continue mixing, about 2–3 minutes. In a small bowl, dissolve instant coffee in hot water and then add to butter mixture. Add sugar, salt, and vanilla, and continue mixing until light and fluffy, about 5 minutes.

Extra Sweets!

Other frosting uses: Vanilla Hazelnut Coffee Pudding (see recipe), frost mocha cupcakes, or mix with crushed shortbread cookies to make a tart crust and fill with vanilla pudding.

Vanilla Hazelnut Coffee Pudding

YIELD: MAKES ABOUT 6–8 ½-CUP SERVINGS

1 box cook-and-serve vanilla pudding
2 cups cold milk
½ cup Hazelnut Coffee Frosting
½ teaspoon cinnamon for garnish
¼ cup hazelnuts for garnish

1. Prepare pudding according to package directions, using the milk as called for. Once the pudding is boiling and before removing from stove, stir in Hazelnut Coffee Frosting until melted.

2. Remove from heat, pour in bowl or individual dishes, and refrigerate to set, about 1 hour or until it's firm. Sprinkle with cinnamon and garnish with a couple of hazelnuts.

Brownie Batter Frosting

YIELD: FROSTS ABOUT 1 DOZEN COOKIES

Traveling home after the Cupcake Wars *showdown was exhausting and our brains just were weren't working—so much so that my assistant extraordinaire, Markie, and I not-so-brilliantly packed a container of cocoa powder into Markie's checked luggage. As each passenger's bag dropped onto the baggage carousel, a puff of brown smoke was released into the air. Soon we were rolling on the baggage claim floor roaring with laughter—especially when Markie's suitcase was finally released . . . completely covered in dark brown cocoa powder. This event was the inspiration for this happiness-inducing Brownie Batter Frosting. And why not: If cocoa makes you laugh, chocolate makes you smile.*

½ cup unsalted butter, softened
¾ cup brown sugar
⅓ cup cocoa powder
¼ cup flour
1 teaspoon pure vanilla extract
½ teaspoon coarse sea salt

In a stand mixer, whip butter and sugar until smooth, about 2 minutes. Add cocoa powder, flour, vanilla, and salt, and whip until light and fluffy, about 5 minutes.

Extra Sweets!

Other frosting uses: Salted Triple Chocolate Brownie Batter Cookies (see recipe); scooped into balls and then rolled in cocoa powder, chopped nuts, or sprinkles to make truffles; or scoop a couple of tablespoons into your favorite milkshake!

Salted Triple Chocolate Brownie Batter Cookies with Brownie Batter Frosting

Salted Triple Chocolate Brownie Batter Cookies

YIELD: 1 DOZEN COOKIES

1 egg yolk
1 batch Brownie Batter Frosting, divided in half
¼ teaspoon baking soda
¼ cup flour
1 cup dark chocolate candy melts
2 teaspoons coarse sea salt

1. Preheat oven to 350°F. In a stand mixer, combine the egg yolk and ½ of the Brownie Batter Frosting and whip until incorporated. Add baking soda and flour, and continue mixing until smooth, about 2 minutes.

2. Scoop tablespoon-sized balls of cookie batter onto a parchment-lined baking sheet and bake for 8–10 minutes. Do not overbake or cookies will be hard.

3. Remove from oven and cool on a cooling rack. Once cool, frost each with a small dollop of the remaining Brownie Batter Frosting.

4. Heat dark chocolate candy melts in the microwave in 30-second intervals until melted and smooth. Carefully spoon about 2 teaspoons of chocolate over each frosted cookie to cover the frosting, then sprinkle with a few crystals of coarse sea salt.

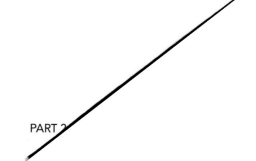

GINGERSNAP STOUT FROSTING

YIELD: MAKES 1 PIE CRUST AND FILLS 1 PIE

Somehow throughout my travels I've become a total beer chick, appreciating the dark notes, the hints of flavors, and the rich and bitter finishes. I've tried to incorporate craft beers into so many frosting recipes that I've had to scold myself to stop. This Gingersnap Stout Frosting, though . . . Oh. My. Gosh. It's a light, creamy, fluffy frosting with bits of gingersnaps and punches of stout that makes the perfect cream filling and the most insanely creative gingersnap crust glue that you'll ever lay witness to. It's intense in theory and just as intense on the tongue.

2 cups unsalted butter, softened
4 teaspoons pure vanilla extract
1 cup stout (not Guinness; I like to use a craft brew, and make sure it's still carbonated)
¼ teaspoon salt
4 cups powdered sugar
40 gingersnaps

In the bowl of a stand mixer, whip the butter until soft, about 2 minutes. Slowly add the vanilla, beer, salt, and sugar, and continue whipping until fluffy, about 4 minutes. In a food processor, finely grind 40 gingersnaps. Add ground gingersnaps to the bowl of frosting and whip until extremely light and fluffy, about 5–7 minutes.

Extra Sweets!

Oth̶e̶r̶ ̶f̶ ̶ ̶ ̶ ̶s: Gingersnap Stout Pie (see recipe), frost
̶ ̶ ̶ ̶es, or gingerbread men.

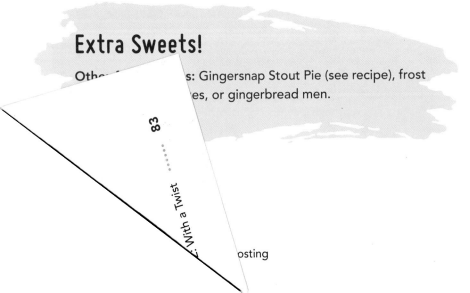

83

With a Twist

osting

Gingersnap Stout Pie

YIELD: MAKES 1 STANDARD PIE

50 gingersnaps
1 batch Gingersnap Stout Frosting (1 cup for the crust plus remainder for the pie filling)
½ cup chocolate frosting for garnish (optional)
½ cup whipped cream for garnish (optional)
3 gingersnaps crushed, plus 1 whole gingersnap for garnish

1. In a food processor, finely grind the gingersnaps, then place in a medium-sized bowl. Add 1 cup of the Gingersnap Stout Frosting and mix until a crumbly cookie crust texture forms (it will resemble a graham cracker pie crust). Press crust firmly into the bottom and sides of a pie tin or 4 or 5 mini pie tins.

2. Preheat oven to 350°F. Put the pie tin in the fridge for about 15 minutes. Remove from fridge and place in oven for another 15 minutes. Remove from oven and allow to cool completely.

3. Scoop remaining Gingersnap Stout Frosting into pie crust and smooth evenly throughout the pie plate. Decorate top with chocolate frosting, whipped cream, and crushed gingersnap crumbs. Place one whole gingersnap in the center and ta-da!

Gingersnap Stout Pie with
Gingersnap Stout Frosting

Chocolate Chipotle
Frosted Nachos with Chili

CHOCOLATE CHIPOTLE FROSTING

YIELD: FROSTS ABOUT 2 DOZEN NACHOS, WITH LEFTOVER FOR DIPPING

You know you need to spice up your social life when you start referring to the animal that lives in your ceiling as your roommate. That's when I turned to making this spicy Chocolate Chipotle Frosting, which is reminiscent of a mole sauce and pairs perfectly with homemade nachos and spicy bean chili. My friends loved the shockingly smoky chipotle frosting, and I had something to brag to my "roommate" about when I returned home after a night out! Kidding! I may need to make more of this frosting and get out of the house more often though . . .

½ cup unsalted butter, softened
1½ teaspoons pure vanilla extract
¼ cup cocoa powder
1½ cups powdered sugar
⅛ teaspoon salt
⅛ teaspoon cinnamon
1 teaspoon chili powder
½ teaspoon chipotle powder
¼ cup hot fudge, left at room temperature (I prefer Mrs. Richardson's)

In the bowl of a stand mixer fitted with the paddle attachment, mix butter until soft about 2 minutes. Slowly add vanilla, cocoa powder, sugar, salt, and spices, and continue mixing another 3–4 minutes. Add fudge and whip until fluffy, about 5 minutes.

Extra Sweets!

Other frosting uses: Chocolate Chipotle Frosted Nachos with Chili (see recipe), as a marinade for chicken, or cinnamon bun frosting.

Chocolate Chipotle Frosted Nachos with Chili

YIELD: MAKES 32–48 NACHOS DEPENDING ON SIZE

1 or 2 rolls of flaky crescent rolls (use more rolls of crescent dough to make more nachos)
1 batch Chocolate Chipotle Frosting
1 can mild chili

1. Preheat oven to 350°F. Open the crescent rolls and separate each dough piece on the dotted line. Some will be larger than others, so you can cut them with a pizza cutter into the shape and size you desire; I like to mix it up and make nachos in different sizes. Take a butter knife or offset spatula and spread a thin layer of frosting on both sides of every piece of dough.

2. Lay pieces of dough on a parchment-lined or sprayed baking sheet, making sure they are not touching each other. Bake in oven for about 12–15 minutes or until they begin to brown. The frosting will spread off the nachos a bit, but don't worry; you can trim that off or leave it for a little extra kick. Remove from the oven and top with chili. Serve warm.

Malbec Ganache Frosting

YIELD: COATS 4 OUNCES OF COOKED PASTA

The greatest thing about this Malbec Ganache Frosting (okay, the second-greatest thing) is how perfectly it morphs into a decadent sauce drizzled over chocolate raspberry pasta, meaning it's a dessert disguised as a meal! Isn't that the best kind of dessert? Now, the greatest thing (truly the greatest this time) is that this Malbec Ganache Frosting only calls for a couple of tablespoons of malbec, which means . . . you guessed it: more for you to drink! A great frosting and a nice glass of wine? The best of both worlds!

½ cup dark chocolate
2 tablespoons malbec

In a small saucepan on medium heat, stir the chocolate until it's fully melted. Add the malbec and continue stirring for about 2 minutes or until smooth. Remove from heat and use immediately while warm. Once it cools it will thicken. If it thickens before you're ready to use it, simply reheat slowly until it's stirrable and smooth again.

Extra Sweets!

Other frosting uses: Chocolate Raspberry Pasta (see recipe), swirl into chocolate cake recipe before baking, or use as a steak marinade.

Chocolate Raspberry Pasta
with Malbec Ganache Frosting

Chocolate Raspberry Pasta

YIELD: ENOUGH FOR 2 LARGE SERVINGS

4 ounces chocolate raspberry pasta (you can buy this from a pasta shop,
    but if you can't find it, regular pasta works, too)
Dash of salt
1 batch Malbec Ganache Frosting
2 tablespoons Raspberry Buttercream (see recipe in Part 1)
½ pint fresh raspberries

1. In a medium saucepan over medium heat, boil the pasta in hot water with a dash of salt.
Once the pasta is al dente, about 5–7 minutes, remove from heat and drain the water.

2. Return the pasta to the medium saucepan, pour the Malbec Ganache Frosting over the
pasta, and stir to coat over low heat. Serve immediately with 1 tablespoon of Raspberry Buttercream and fresh raspberries on each serving.

STRAWBERRY MERINGUE FROSTING

YIELD: MAKES ABOUT 4 CUPS

I can hear you now, "Meringue? Isn't that a cookie?" Well, meringue is first and foremost a frosting; however, its unique combination of egg whites and sugar, whipped to perfect peaks, lends itself well to being baked into cookie form. This delicious, baked Strawberry Meringue Frosting is absolutely amazing when you add fresh strawberries and a few sprinkles of finely chopped dark chocolate to create a porous, cloudlike, crumbless cookie that just begs to be dropped in a tall goblet of stout . . . yes, stout. Trust me. You won't regret it!

4 egg whites
1½ cups white sugar
1 teaspoon cream of tartar

⅛ teaspoon salt
1½ teaspoons pure vanilla extract
3 medium strawberries

1. Add the egg whites, sugar, cream of tartar, and salt to a double boiler over simmering water and whisk quickly and continually until they become very white and slightly bubbly, about 5–6 minutes.

2. Immediately remove egg mixture from double boiler and quickly scrape into the bowl of your stand mixer fitted with the whisk attachment. Add vanilla. Mix on high approximately 9 minutes, until soft peaks form. Process 3 medium-sized strawberries in your food processor or finely chop by hand. Gently fold chopped strawberries into meringue with a spatula.

Extra Sweets!

Other frosting uses: Floating Strawberry Meringue Drop Cookies (see recipe), as the topping to strawberry cream pie, or top angel food cake and serve with a side of strawberries.

Floating Strawberry
Meringue Drop Cookies
with Strawberry
Meringue Frosting

Floating Strawberry Meringue Drop Cookies

YIELD: ABOUT 24 SMALL COOKIES

¼ cup dark chocolate, chopped

1 batch Strawberry Meringue Frosting

1–4 tall glasses of chocolate stout to drop your cookies into, depending on how many people are drinking with you (No shame if you're drinking alone.)

1. Preheat oven to 350°F. Gently fold ¼ cup dark chocolate into the Strawberry Meringue Frosting. Drop ½ tablespoon dollops of Meringue onto a greased cookie sheet and bake for 25 minutes or until they become firm. They will spread, so make sure you leave enough room between each cookie.

2. Remove from oven and allow to cool. Gently scrape each cookie off the cookie sheet; they have a tendency to break and crackle here so be gentle. Drop one in the bottom of a beer glass, pour a chocolate stout slowly on top, and watch your cookie rise like the royal ship of the beer seas.

Margarita Meringue Frosting

YIELD: MAKES ABOUT 4 CUPS

I know I'm not going to win any fans with the secret I'm about to divulge, but I feel you all should know the truth: I don't like margaritas. I know, I know, how can I, the lover and developer of such sweet creations, the gal who can live on frosted cookies alone, not appreciate a sugary drink? Since I can see you scowling at me right now, perhaps I can win back your affections with this delectable Margarita Meringue Frosting? Make this frosting if you too don't like drinking your sweets yet still want to shout "olé" at the Mexican fiesta.

4 egg whites
1½ cups white sugar
⅛ teaspoon salt
1 teaspoon cream of tartar

3 teaspoons tequila
1 teaspoon Cointreau
Zest and juice of 1 lime

1. Add the egg whites, sugar, salt, and cream of tartar to a double boiler over simmering water and whisk quickly and continually until they become very white and slightly bubbly, about 5–6 minutes.

2. Immediately remove egg-white mixture from double boiler and scrape into the bowl of your stand mixer fitted with the whisk attachment. Mix on high approximately 9 minutes, until soft peaks form.

3. Add in tequila, Cointreau, lime zest, and lime juice and whip 1 more minute, until liquids have been well incorporated. For a stronger liquor taste, add more tequila.

Extra Sweets!

Other frosting uses: Margarita Crispy Rice Treats (see recipe), dip the rim of your margarita glasses in the meringue before dipping them in coarse salt, or add to a frozen margarita before blending for a sweet change.

Margarita Crispy Rice Treats
with Margarita Meringue Frosting

Margarita Crispy Rice Treats

YIELD: MAKES ONE 8" × 8" PAN

4 tablespoons butter

5 ounces large marshmallows

1 batch Margarita Meringue Frosting (reserve 2 tablespoons for garnish)

1 lime cut into wedges for garnish

Zest of 2 limes

4 cups Rice Krispies

Coarse margarita or sea salt

1. Melt butter and large marshmallows in a pot over medium heat. Stir until marshmallows are melted and smooth. Add the Margarita Meringue Frosting (setting 2 tablespoons aside for garnish) and continue stirring until everything is blended and sticky. You may have to reduce the heat so that the marshmallows don't burn. Add in the zest of 1½ limes, stir to incorporate, and then remove from heat.

2. Spray a bowl and spatula with cooking spray. Place Rice Krispies in the bowl and pour the marshmallow mixture on top. Mix until fully combined. I like my treats to be super gooey, but if this is too sticky for you, just add a few more Rice Krispies. When you're happy with your Meringue-to-cereal ratio, spread the mixture evenly into a liberally sprayed 8" × 8" pan. Sprinkle the tops with a couple pinches of coarse margarita salt or sea salt and the zest of the remaining half of the lime. Allow to set before cutting into squares. Serve in margarita glasses with a dollop of Margarita Meringue frosting and a lime wedge for that real fiesta feeling.

Strawberry Champagne Frosting

YIELD: FROSTS ABOUT 3 DOZEN CAKE BITES

Honestly, I'm not sure if I'll ever get married, and if I did, the only real reason for me to have a big wedding would be to put this celebratory Strawberry Champagne Frosting on top of, well, everything. And I'm not alone. Wedding consultations at Dollop always (and I mean always*) consisted of a bride ~~asking~~ pleading to try my effervescent, pink-hued Strawberry Champagne Frosting. When a groom-to-be confides he only tagged along to try this frosting, you know you have a hit on your hands. And if you're like me and unsure of a future of marital bliss, this bubbly frosting is suitable for all celebrations! Enjoy!*

½ cup unsalted butter
1½ cups powdered sugar
Pinch of salt
1 tablespoon vanilla extract
2 tablespoons strawberry champagne
1 fresh raspberry

Whip butter in the bowl of a stand mixer fitted with a paddle attachment until soft, about 2 minutes. Slowly add sugar, salt, vanilla, and strawberry champagne to the bowl and mix until blended, about 4 minutes. Add the raspberry and mix again another 2–3 minutes until light and fluffy. Voilà, pink Strawberry Champagne Frosting!

Extra Sweets!

Other frosting uses: Champagne Cake Bites with Raspberries (see recipe); squeeze ½ tablespoon into ice cube trays, press a raspberry inside, and freeze for an hour; or make mini champagne cupcakes and dollop on top.

Champagne Cake Bites
with Raspberries and Strawberry
Champagne Frosting

Champagne Cake Bites with Raspberries

YIELD: MAKES ABOUT 3 DOZEN

⅓ cup unsalted butter
¾ cup white sugar
¼ teaspoon vanilla
1½ cups flour
½ tablespoon baking powder
½ teaspoon salt

½ cup strawberry champagne
3 egg whites
1 pint raspberries
1 batch Strawberry Champagne Frosting
2 tablespoons raw sugar or colored sanding
   sugar, for garnish

1. Preheat oven to 250°F. In the bowl of a stand mixer fitted with the paddle attachment, mix butter and sugar about 2 minutes. Add the vanilla and continuing mixing for 2 minutes, until blended. In a separate small bowl, whisk together flour, baking powder, and salt. Add flour mixture to butter mixture, alternating with the champagne, until all ingredients are fully incorporated. Transfer to a separate bowl and wash out the bowl of the stand mixer and fit it with the whisk attachment.

2. Whip egg whites in the stand mixer until they get foamy and soft peaks form, about 3 minutes. Gently fold the egg whites into the batter.

3. Cover the bottom of a 9" × 13" baking pan with parchment paper and spray the sides with non-stick cooking spray. Spread the cake batter evenly into the pan so that it's about ½" thick. Press half the raspberries into the batter, in rows (reserve the other half of the raspberries to decorate the tops of the finished cake bites). Place in the oven and bake for about 20–22 minutes, or until a toothpick inserted in the center comes out clean. Remove cake from oven and allow to cool fully on a cooling rack.

4. Once cool, take a small circle cookie cutter and cut cake circles, and then gently pop them out of the pan. Dollop each with Strawberry Champagne Frosting, a sprinkling of raw sugar or colored sanding sugar, and a fresh raspberry, and serve! You'll have cake scraps left over that can be used to make cake balls, cake and frosting trifles, or cake snacks to shove in your mouth when you just need something sweet.

PART 3

~ Be Crazy: ~
LIVE A FROSTED LIFE

I'm the girl who sets the oven timer yet forgets to put the cake in the oven. The speaker who writes the perfect speech yet doesn't remember to print it. The businesswoman who builds a business from scratch yet shuts it down at its height. Crazy, right? Are you in need of some crazy inspiration? You've come to the right place! The deliciously crazy frosting recipes found in this part will have you twirling through the delight of your own creativity, inspiration, and faith in the unknown. Whether you're craving frosting infused with spices or sweets packed with hip fancy cheeses, these crazy frostings have it all. The Juniper Chocolate Frosting will make you want to frolic in snow banks, while the Peach Basil Whipped Cream will make you want to invite your entire city over for pancakes (which I strongly caution you against doing). So grab the craziest ingredients you can think of, update your Facebook status to "I'm getting crazy with frosting!," and let's start living this crazy, frosted life already!

LAVENDER ORANGE FROSTING

YIELD: FROSTS 1 LOAF OF BISCOTTI

Do you remember the 1980s commercial where a man rolled down the window of his Rolls-Royce to ask, "Pardon me, do you have any Grey Poupon?" That man inspired this lovely Lavender Orange Frosting. Let me explain. In my imagination I'm rolling around in my Rolls-Royce seeking out a dainty cup of tea (much better than spicy mustard). As I careen through the lush, green hills I can smell the refreshing aroma of fresh lavender and orange blossoms wafting through the air. Voilà! A Lavender Orange Frosting would make the perfect Earl Grey pairing! And that's *how this deliciousness came to be!*

½ cup unsalted butter, softened
2 cups powdered sugar
Pinch of salt
1 teaspoon pure vanilla extract
½ teaspoon orange extract or the zest of 1 orange
2 teaspoons dried lavender

In the bowl of a stand mixer fitted with the paddle attachment, cream butter until smooth, about 2 minutes. Add sugar, salt, vanilla, orange zest, and lavender, and continue mixing until light and fluffy, about 5 minutes.

Extra Sweets!

Other frosting uses: Lavender Orange Biscotti (see recipe), dollop on lemon tarts, or serve alongside pound cake.

Lavender Orange
Biscotti with Lavender
Orange Frosting

Lavender Orange Biscotti

YIELD: MAKES ABOUT 18 BISCOTTI

3 eggs
¼ cup olive oil
¾ cup sugar
½ cup Lavender Orange Frosting plus 1 cup to frost biscotti
3¼ cups flour
1 tablespoon baking powder
Zest of one orange
2 teaspoons lavender

1. Preheat oven to 375°F. In the bowl of a stand mixer fitted with a paddle attachment, mix eggs and olive oil about 1 minute, until blended. Add sugar and continue mixing for 2 minutes. Add ½ cup Lavender Orange Frosting and beat until the lumps smooth out. Add flour and baking powder and continue mixing until heavy dough forms, about 4–5 minutes.

2. Split the dough in half and roll each half into a log about a foot long. Each loaf will make about 10–12 biscotti, so you can bake both or wrap one in plastic wrap and place it in the freezer for a later time.

3. Press 1 loaf into ½" thickness on a parchment-lined baking sheet. Sprinkle the top with ½ of the orange zest and 1 teaspoon lavender. Bake for 25 minutes or until the loaf just starts to brown very slightly. Remove from oven and let cool for about 10–15 minutes.

4. Next, gently slice the loaf into 1" slices (this is when it starts to resemble biscotti as you know it). Take a butter knife and smear a thin layer of Lavender Orange Frosting onto each side of each slice, place them one frosted side down on the baking sheet, and bake an additional 6 minutes.

5. Remove from oven, flip each slice over so the other frosted side is down, and bake another 6 minutes. Remove from oven and allow to cool. Serve with Earl Grey tea or even some orange blossom beer!

HONEY BRIE FROSTING

YIELD: FROSTS ABOUT 24 COOKIES

Sometimes—and I'm slightly afraid to admit this—I envy the hipsters. Their scientific coffee, green eco-clothing, mustachioed swagger, and artistic soirees make me feel as though I'm on the fringe of greatness when I read of their successes in the local papers. This Honey Brie Frosting feels warm yet edgy enough to maybe, just maybe, eke me into the hipster crowd for just one night. After all, why wouldn't you want to feel like all eyes and artistic souls are on you for an evening?

4 ounces cream cheese, softened
¼ cup unsalted butter, softened
4 ounces Brie, softened
1 cup powdered sugar
2 teaspoons honey

In the bowl of a stand mixer fitted with whisk attachment, whip cream cheese until smooth. Add butter and continuing mixing, about 3 minutes or until smooth. Add Brie and whip about another 3 minutes, until smooth. Add sugar and mix until smooth. Add honey and mix for about 2 minutes, until creamy and smooth.

Extra Sweets!

Other frosting uses: Rosemary Sea Salt Shortbreads with Fig (see recipe), as the sauce on a pizza topped with fresh figs and green apples before baking, or spread on crostini drizzled with honey and balsamic and sprinkled with chopped pistachios.

Rosemary Sea Salt Shortbreads
with Fig and Honey Brie Frosting

PHOTO BY MATT DETURCK

Rosemary Sea Salt Shortbreads with Fig

YIELD: MAKES ABOUT 24 COOKIES

1 cup unsalted butter
½ cup white sugar
½ egg
2 teaspoons pure vanilla extract
2 teaspoons dried rosemary plus ½ teaspoon to press into cookies
3½ cups flour
½ teaspoon coarse sea salt
1 batch Honey Brie Frosting
¼ cup fig preserves

1. In the bowl of a stand mixer fitted with a paddle attachment, cream the butter and sugar, about 3 minutes. Add the egg and continue mixing for another 1–2 minutes. Add vanilla, 2 teaspoons rosemary, and flour, and mix until a thick dough forms, about 5 minutes. Divide the dough in half and roll into 2 logs, each about 3" in diameter. Freeze the logs for 1 hour.

2. Preheat oven to 375°F. Remove logs from freezer and slice in ¼"-thick round slices. Lay the cookies flat and press a very tiny pinch of rosemary and a very tiny pinch of coarse sea salt into the tops of each cookie. Arrange on a parchment-lined baking sheet and bake for 8–10 minutes, or just before they barely start browning on the edge. Remove from oven.

3. Allow cookies to cool, then frost with a dollop of Honey Brie Frosting and garnish with a smidgen of fig preserves.

White Chocolate Blueberry Ganache

YIELD: MAKES ABOUT 30 COOKIES

This guy I know whom I won't name (Dan) wears a purple shirt so often that one day I decided I needed to make a frosting to match him (because that would be funny, right?). To my delight, I was able to create the most glorious deep purple hue that perfectly matched his favorite button-down shirt—just like a bridesmaid dyes her shoes to match her dress! He didn't find my humor as charming as I did, but he did quickly devour this White Chocolate Blueberry Ganache. And you will, too!

½ cup heavy cream
1 cup blueberries
10 ounces white chocolate chips

In a medium saucepot over medium heat, stir heavy cream and blueberries, continuously whisking until mixture starts to boil. Place chocolate chips in a separate medium bowl. Mash the blueberries with your whisk while stirring as they begin to soften. Once boiling, pour mixture over the white chocolate. Whisk until completely smooth and chocolate is melted, then set aside to cool.

Extra Sweets!

Other frosting uses: Pear Cookies (see recipe), swirl into cheesecake filling before pouring into the crust and baking, or fill mini chocolate cups for a blueberry dessert "shot."

Pear Cookies with White
Chocolate Blueberry Ganache

Pear Cookies

YIELD: MAKES ABOUT 30 COOKIES

2½ cups flour
2 teaspoons baking powder
Pinch of salt
½ cup butter
1 cup brown sugar
2 eggs
1 batch White Chocolate Blueberry Ganache (½ cup for dough, remainder for frosting)
1 cup diced Bosc pear
30 blueberries

1. Preheat oven to 375°F. Sift flour, baking powder, and salt in bowl and set aside. In the bowl of a stand mixer fitted with a paddle attachment, cream butter with brown sugar, about 2–3 minutes. Add eggs and continue mixing until blended, about 1 minute. Alternate adding flour mixture and the ½ cup White Chocolate Blueberry Ganache until completely incorporated. Mix in 1 cup diced pears.

2. Scoop cookies onto a parchment-lined baking sheet with a small ice cream scoop and bake for 12–15 minutes, until no longer gooey in the center and edges begin to brown. Allow cookies to cool.

3. Frost cookies with remainder of White Chocolate Blueberry Ganache and top with 1 blueberry each.

Orange Cardamom Icing

YIELD: FROSTS ABOUT 1–2 DOZEN COOKIES

Inspired by the Hanukkah cookie making I used to do once a year as a kid, this Orange Cardamom Icing adds a little extra something to spice up those traditional (i.e., boring) holiday cookies. Tint this frosting the colors of the rainbow and use it to festively decorate your cookies this season. From Christmas to Kwanzaa to Valentine's Day, this flavorful frosting will be the gift that keeps on giving.

1 cup powdered sugar
1 tablespoon almond milk
⅛ teaspoon cream of tartar
1 teaspoon vanilla
¼ teaspoon orange extract or zest of 1 orange
⅛ teaspoon cardamom
6–8 drops food coloring, color of your choice (optional)

Mix all ingredients in a medium bowl until pasty. If desired, add your choice of food coloring, or divide into separate bowls to make multiple colors. For a thicker frosting, add more powdered sugar, 1 tablespoon at a time, until you reach your desired consistency.

Extra Sweets!

Other frosting uses: Orange Cut-Out Cookies (see recipe), glaze on gingerbread muffins, or drizzle over pumpkin donuts.

Orange Cut-Out Cookies with
Orange Cardamom Icing

Orange Cut-Out Cookies

YIELD: MAKES ABOUT 24 COOKIES

1 cup butter
1 egg
1 teaspoon pure vanilla extract
1 teaspoon orange extract or zest of 1 orange
1½ cups powdered sugar
2½ cups flour
1 teaspoon baking soda
1 teaspoon raw sugar
1 batch Orange Cardamom Icing

1. In the bowl of your stand mixer fitted with the paddle attachment, cream butter until smooth, about 2 minutes. Add egg, vanilla, and orange extract or zest, and mix until incorporated. Add sugar, flour, and baking soda, and continue mixing until heavy dough forms, about 5 minutes. Split dough in half, roll each half in a ball, and place in freezer for 1 hour.

2. Preheat oven to 375°F. Remove dough from freezer; roll out on parchment paper until about ¼" thick. Cut with desired cookie cutters, sprinkle with raw sugar, place on parchment-lined baking sheet, and bake for 8–10 minutes. Remove from oven and let cool. Decorate with Orange Cardamom Icing, and allow icing to firm before stacking or storing.

 CLOVE BUTTERCREAM

YIELD: FROSTS ABOUT 3 DOZEN CUPCAKES

The balance between the clove and cinnamon in this Clove Buttercream is what got me crowned Cupcake Wars champion! In round one, we had to create one cupcake using any three of a table's worth of surprise ingredients that included barbecue sauce, mustard, beef jerky, clove, beer, bittersweet chocolate, cayenne pepper, and anchovies. Talk about a challenge! I came up with this Clove Buttercream and used it to top a brown sugar beer cake dipped in a bittersweet hard chocolate shell and topped with a spicy chocolate beer caramel. Initially, I went overboard on the clove in the frosting and almost got sent home, but the judges gave me another chance and asked me to remake this frosting in round three. Victory ensued!

2 cups unsalted butter
½ cup butter-flavored shortening
2 tablespoons pure vanilla extract
6½ cups confectioners' sugar
Pinch of salt
2 teaspoons ground clove
1 teaspoon ground cinnamon

Cream butter and shortening together by placing them in the mixing bowl fitted with the paddle attachment and mixing on low speed, about 2 minutes until smooth. Add vanilla and continue mixing another minute. Sift sugar in a bowl to get rid of any lumps, and add salt. Slowly add sugar 1 cup at a time to butter mixture, scraping down bowl in between additions until all of the sugar is incorporated, about 3 minutes. Add clove and cinnamon, and continuing mixing until frosting is light and fluffy, about 5 minutes.

Extra Sweets!

Other frosting uses: Bittersweet Chocolate, Clove, Beer, and Spicy Beer Caramel Cupcakes (see recipe); frost blueberry coffee cake; dollop on mini star anise cookies.

Bittersweet Chocolate,
Clove, Beer, and Spicy
Beer Caramel Cupcakes
with Clove Buttercream

Bittersweet Chocolate, Clove, Beer, and Spicy Beer Caramel Cupcakes

YIELD: ABOUT 1 DOZEN CUPCAKES

For Cupcakes

3 tablespoons unsalted butter
1 cup light brown sugar, packed
2 eggs
1½ cups all-purpose flour
1 teaspoon baking powder
½ teaspoon baking soda
Pinch of salt
12 ounces black wheat beer

For cupcakes: Preheat the oven to 350°F. Line a cupcake or muffin pan with 12 cupcake liners. Cream the butter and light brown sugar together by placing it in the mixing bowl fitted with the paddle attachment and mix on low speed, about 2 minutes until smooth. Scrape down the sides of the bowl and then add 1 egg at a time, scraping down the sides of the bowl after each addition. Mix the dry ingredients together in a separate bowl. Add the dry ingredients and the beer, alternating between the two, beginning and ending with the dry ingredients. Fill the 12 cupcake liners ¾ full with batter and bake for 18 minutes, or until a toothpick inserted into the center comes out clean. Cool the cupcakes completely.

For Bittersweet Chocolate Shell

1 cup dark chocolate candy melts
¼ cup bittersweet chocolate shavings

For bittersweet chocolate shell: Put the dark chocolate candy melts and the bittersweet chocolate shavings in a microwave-safe bowl and microwave in 30-second intervals 3 times or until fully melted. Dip each cupcake one at a time upside down in the chocolate mixture so just the tops of the cupcakes are thinly coated in chocolate. Set the cupcakes aside for the chocolate to cool and harden. Reserve the remaining chocolate mixture for the Spicy Beer Caramels.

For Spicy Beer Caramels (optional)

1 cup granulated sugar
¼ cup corn syrup
1 cup black wheat beer
1 tablespoon unsalted butter
½ tablespoon cayenne pepper
½ tablespoon chili powder
Pinch of habanero, ground
1½ teaspoons baking soda
1 teaspoon sea salt

For Spicy Beer Caramels (optional): Line a half sheet tray with wax paper and set aside. Combine granulated sugar, corn syrup, beer, butter, cayenne pepper, chili powder, and habanero in a heavy saucepan and heat over medium heat, stirring occasionally for 30 minutes or until a candy thermometer reads 225°F. Remove from heat and stir in baking soda and sea salt. Mixture will thicken, bubble, and turn opaque. Pour mixture on the prepared sheet tray and place in the freezer. Remove sheet tray once mixture thickens to a sticky, caramel consistency. Take a plastic chocolate candy mold and scoop in about ¼ teaspoon of the reserved bittersweet chocolate mixture. Then scoop in ¼ teaspoon of Spicy Beer Caramel, and cover with another small scoop of bittersweet chocolate shell. Place in the freezer to harden.

For Assembly

1 batch Clove Buttercream
½ cup bittersweet chocolate, chopped

To assemble: Take a chocolate-dipped cupcake and frost generously with a dollop of Clove Buttercream. Crumble bittersweet chocolate on top. Place a Spicy Beer Caramel on top. These can be fairly time consuming so they're completely optional in the making of this awesome cupcake. The finished cupcakes are wholly delicious with or without the spicy beer caramel on top!

Strawberry Balsamic Goat Cheese Frosting

YIELD: MAKES 6 MINI CHEESECAKES

I refuse to eat lunch. The thought of tomato soup at noon or pepperoni pizza at 1 P.M. sends my anxiety soaring. That's why this Strawberry Balsamic Goat Cheese Frosting is so revolutionary! It's like cheese and fruit—in frosting form. Even better, the Strawberry Balsamic Reduction can double as a salad dressing for dinner. Yum!

For Strawberry Balsamic Reduction

YIELD: ABOUT 1 CUP

1¼ cups fresh strawberries
2 tablespoons brown sugar
2 tablespoons balsamic vinegar

For Frosting

½ cup cream cheese, softened
½ cup goat cheese, softened
¼ cup brown sugar
¼ teaspoons salt
3 tablespoons Strawberry Balsamic Reduction

1. **For Strawberry Balsamic Reduction:** In a medium saucepot over low heat, cook ingredients until reduced, stirring frequently, for about 45–50 minutes. Remove from heat, pour in a bowl, and allow to cool.

2. **For the frosting:** In the bowl of a stand mixer fitted with a paddle attachment, mix cream cheese until smooth. Add goat cheese and continue mixing about 4–5 minutes, until smooth. Scrape sides and bottom of bowl and mix again until smooth. Add sugar, salt, and Strawberry Balsamic Reduction, and mix until fully incorporated. Scrape sides and bottom of bowl and mix until frosting is smooth and creamy, about 1–2 minutes.

Extra Sweets!

Other frosting uses: Strawberry Spinach Cheesecakes (see recipe); spread on French bread, topped with prosciutto, and toasted; or tossed with spinach, craisins, strawberries, toasted pecans, and roasted figs.

Strawberry Spinach Cheesecakes with Strawberry Balsamic Goat Cheese Frosting

Strawberry Spinach Cheesecakes

YIELD: MAKES 6 MINI CHEESECAKES

FOR CHEESECAKE FILLING

¼ cup Greek yogurt
½ cup sour cream
1 tablespoon cornstarch
1 batch Strawberry Balsamic Goat Cheese Frosting

FOR SPINACH PECAN CRUST

1 cup unsalted pecans, ground
½ cup raw spinach, chopped
2 tablespoons brown sugar
1 tablespoon unsalted butter, melted
Pinch of salt

FOR GARNISH: STRAWBERRY BALSAMIC REDUCTION

(see recipe for Strawberry Balsamic Goat Cheese Frosting)

1. For cheesecake filling: Add yogurt, sour cream, and cornstarch to the Strawberry Balsamic Goat Cheese Frosting and mix until well combined.

2. For spinach pecan crust: Preheat oven to 350°F. Chop nuts in food processor; add spinach and continue processing until smooth, about 1–2 minutes. Add sugar, melted butter, and salt. Process until well combined and thick, about 20 seconds. Do not over chop because the mixture will become juice. Line a baking tin with paper liners and press 2 tablespoons of crust mixture into each cupcake mold. Make sure it's well packed in the bottom. Bake for 15 minutes, or until browned and firm looking.

3. To assemble: Remove crusts from oven and spoon cheesecake filling over crusts until almost full. Fill a roasting pan about ⅓ full of water and place the cupcake tin inside so it's floating. Bake for 20–25 minutes. The cheesecakes should start to look firmer on top. Remove from oven and allow to cool completely. Once cool, place in fridge for an hour to firm up, then served chilled with a spoonful of Strawberry Balsamic Reduction over each.

Juniper Chocolate Frosting

Sometimes I feel a bit crazy from being cooped up during the cold winter in upstate New York. Fortunately, a whiff of this Juniper Chocolate Frosting is a reminder of a peaceful, quiet frolic through freshly fallen snow. Smeared on some Blackberry Brownies, this frosting helps you to close your eyes and imagine yourself standing alone on an island of icing. The fact that your friends will be enamored with this wintry berry burst will just be a bonus. Funny how the craziest frosting concoctions have an uncanny ability to create a sense of calm in your mind . . .

1 cup unsalted butter, softened
½ cup sweetened condensed milk
2 teaspoons pure vanilla extract
4 tablespoons cocoa powder
1 teaspoon ground juniper berries

In the bowl of a stand mixer fitted with the whisk attachment, beat butter about 2 minutes until creamy. Add condensed milk, vanilla, cocoa, and juniper berries, and continue beating until soft and fluffy, about 5 minutes.

Extra Sweets!

Other frosting uses: Blackberry Brownies (see recipe), dollop on a mixed-berry tart, or scoop a couple of tablespoons on baked apples and serve with a gin and tonic.

Blackberry Brownies with
Juniper Chocolate Frosting

Blackberry Brownies

YIELD: MAKES 1 8" × 8" PAN OF BROWNIES

2 cups granulated sugar
4 eggs
1 cup unsalted butter, melted
3 teaspoons pure vanilla extract
½ cup cocoa powder
1 cup flour
½ teaspoon salt
½ teaspoon baking powder
1 pint fresh blackberries
1 batch Juniper Chocolate Frosting

1. Preheat oven to 375°F. In the bowl of a stand mixer fitted with a paddle attachment, beat sugar, eggs, melted butter, and vanilla, about 1 minute. Add cocoa, flour, salt, and baking powder, and continue mixing until combined.

2. Pour batter into an 8" × 8" greased brownie pan. Press blackberries into the batter in rows. Bake for 25–30 minutes or until a toothpick inserted in the center comes out clean. Remove from oven and allow to cool before frosting with the Juniper Chocolate Frosting.

PEACH BASIL WHIPPED CREAM

YIELD: MAKES ABOUT 2 CUPS

My dad is a whipped cream fanatic. He'll even close his eyes while tasting it, like he's being transported to a decadent whipped cream world where fluffy, creamy sweetness reigns supreme. I, on the other hand, am not a huge fan, which is why I needed to create this seductively sweet Peach Basil Whipped Cream. Just thinking about it will make you want to close your eyes and experience my dad's heavenly whipped cream world!

PEACH BASIL SAUCE

4 tablespoons unsalted butter
1 cup packed brown sugar
1 cup fresh basil, chopped
1 cup peach slices, fresh or frozen

WHIPPED CREAM

¾ cup heavy cream
1–2 teaspoons bourbon (optional)

1. **To make the Peach Basil Sauce:** In a cast-iron or nonstick skillet over medium heat, cook butter, sugar, basil, and peaches, stirring continuously for about 20 minutes or until it thickens. Remove from heat and allow to cool.

2. **To make the whipped cream:** In a chilled bowl of a stand mixer fitted with a whisk attachment, whip heavy cream on high speed until thick, about 6–9 minutes. Add the bourbon (if you're hardcore) and mix an additional 30 seconds.

3. **To combine:** Add 2 tablespoons of the cooled Peach Basil Sauce to the whipped cream and whip 1 minute until just incorporated. The volume will go down slightly, but you don't want to overmix at this point, you just want the peach and basil peeking through.

Extra Sweets!

Other frosting uses: Peach Basil Pancakes (see recipe), dollop atop pecan pie and vanilla bean ice cream, or top a hot toddy or warm cider.

Peach Basil Pancakes with Peach Basil Whipped Cream

Peach Basil Pancakes

YIELD: MAKES ABOUT 12 SMALLISH PANCAKES

1 cup flour
1 teaspoon baking powder
½ teaspoon baking soda
¼ teaspoon salt
1 egg
1 cup buttermilk
½ cup Peach Basil Sauce plus extra for garnish (optional)
½ cup Peach Basil Whipped Cream

1. In a mixing bowl, whisk together flour, baking powder, baking soda, salt, egg, and buttermilk. Add Peach Basil Sauce and mix until evenly distributed.

2. In a cast-iron skillet or a nonstick pan sprayed with cooking spray over low heat, carefully ladle pancake batter a couple of tablespoons at a time into the center. The more batter, the bigger the pancake. I like to keep my pancakes smaller because they're easier to flip and I can make more. Let the pancake cook about 1–2 minutes and then carefully flip it onto the other side and allow it to cook 1–2 minutes more. Remove from pan and place on a plate while you continue ladling the rest of the batter. You can place the pancakes on a foil-lined baking tray in a 200°F oven to keep warm while you finish cooking the rest of the pancakes.

3. Stack pancakes, scoop Peach Basil Whipped Cream over top, and finish with a drizzle of Peach Basil Sauce, if desired.

Cashew Sriracha Frosting

This spicy Cashew Sriracha Frosting made its debut appearance at a similarly spicy lingerie party thrown by the young professional crowd. While the ladies were perusing the lacy bras and cheeky panties, the men were delving into my delicious, frosted snacks. When one of the men excitedly approached me, asking where he could buy this frosting, I knew it was something more than special. So, sir, I hope you're still dreaming of this sweetly spicy, crunchy, nutty frosting because here's the recipe! Have fun!

3 cups roasted cashews, unsalted
1 cup unsalted butter, softened
2 cups powdered sugar
Pinch of salt
3 tablespoons sriracha

1. Process the cashews in a food processor until they reach a butterlike consistency, about 5–10 minutes. You might have to stop the processor periodically and scrape the sides and bottom to keep the nuts moving around.

2. Whip butter in stand mixer until smooth. Add ground cashews and continue mixing 1–2 minutes, scraping down sides and bottom of the bowl to make sure it's all incorporated. Add in powdered sugar and salt, and continue whipping until light and fluffy, about 2 minutes. Slowly mix in the sriracha to desired heat.

Extra Sweets!

Other frosting uses: Sriracha Brownies (see recipe), put a couple of tablespoons in a pan with some chicken and sauté away, or use as a filling in chocolate candy bar molds to make your own kickin' candy bars.

Sriracha Brownies
with Cashew
Sriracha Frosting

Sriracha Brownies

YIELD: MAKES 1 9" × 13" PAN OF BROWNIES

1 cup unsalted butter, melted
2 cups white sugar
4 eggs
⅔ cup cocoa powder
1 cup flour
½ teaspoon salt
½ teaspoon baking powder
⅔ cup chocolate chips
2 tablespoons sriracha
1 cup Cashew Sriracha Frosting plus remainder to frost tops of brownies (optional)

1. Preheat oven to 350°F. In the bowl of a stand mixer, add butter, sugar, and eggs, and mix until incorporated. Add cocoa, flour, salt, and baking powder, and continue blending another 2–3 minutes. Scrape down sides and bottom of bowl. Add chocolate chips and sriracha, and mix until all ingredients are evenly combined.

2. Spread the brownie batter in a 9" × 13" pan that has been sprayed with cooking spray or lined with parchment paper.

3. Swirl 1 cup of the Cashew Sriracha Frosting through the brownie batter with a butter knife. Bake for 35–40 minutes or until a toothpick inserted into the center comes out clean. Let cool before cutting. Want your brownies extra frosted? Use the remainder of frosting to spread on top of the brownies!

Coconut Almond Frosting

YIELD: MAKES ABOUT 3 CUPS

There are times that I've just returned from working my butt off at the gym and all I crave is a delicious bowl of frosting. I'm not alone here, am I? Always one to go after my goals, I developed this paleo Coconut Almond Frosting that can be devoured postworkout, guilt free! Well, kinda, sorta guilt free—which is close enough. Even better, it tastes amazing, lacks refined sugar, and packs a big dose of protein from the almonds. Add in some oats and dark chocolate and you're just upping the antioxidant and yum factor simultaneously. Don't blame me if you start loving how your butt looks in those jeans again!

1 tablespoon arrowroot
1 cup coconut palm sugar
1 cup raw almonds
1 teaspoon pure vanilla extract
1 teaspoon water

1 cup unsalted butter or refined coconut oil, softened
¼ teaspoon salt
2 tablespoons cocoa powder
¼ cup dark chocolate (optional)

In a food processor, blend arrowroot with coconut palm sugar until well mixed, then empty into small bowl. In the same food processor, blend almonds, adding vanilla and water until buttery, about 5–10 minutes. Cream butter or coconut oil until soft by placing it in the mixing bowl fitted with the paddle attachment and mix on low speed about 4 minutes. Add almonds and continue mixing for 2 minutes. Add sugar/arrowroot mixture, salt, and cocoa, and continue mixing another 2 minutes. Add chopped chocolate, if desired.

Extra Sweets!

Other frosting uses: Cashew Chocolate Bacon Bark (see recipe), as a frosting on your favorite gluten-free chocolate cake, spread on an English muffin topped with cooked egg whites and honeyed ham, or mix with cooked sweet potatoes to make a creamy "mashed" sweet potato.

Cashew Chocolate Bacon Bark

YIELD: 2–3 CUPS

5 strips thick-cut bacon
1 cup Coconut Almond Frosting
1 cup raw cashews

1. Preheat oven to 400°F. Cook bacon to desired crispiness. Remove bacon and chop into pieces.

2. In a medium-sized bowl, mix bacon, Coconut Almond Frosting, and cashews.

3. Spread mixture evenly onto a parchment-lined baking sheet. Bake for 6–8 minutes or until it's bubbling; don't let it burn. Remove from oven, allow to cool, and either break into pieces or crumble.

Cashew Chocolate Bacon Bark with Coconut Almond Frosting

Tahini Currant Crispy Rice Bars with Tahini Currant Frosting

Tahini Currant Frosting

YIELD: MAKES ABOUT 2 CUPS

A desire to develop a frosting that I could proudly tote to my gluten-free CrossFit coaches is what truly inspired this Tahini Currant Frosting. The unique flavor of tahini mixed with dark chocolate and currants, all combined nicely, is a surprise for the senses and a delight to those on a gluten-free diet. There's not much "bad" going on here other than your desire to eat the whole bowl—in one sitting. Not that there's anything wrong with that . . .

½ cup tahini paste
2 cups Rice Chex
2 tablespoons raw agave nectar
2 tablespoons currants
½ teaspoon pure vanilla extract
½ cup coconut palm sugar
½ cup dark chocolate, melted

In a large bowl, mix all ingredients together until well incorporated. This is a chunkier style frosting due to the Rice Chex, so mix until large pieces are broken up and texture is that of a chunky nut butter.

Extra Sweets!

Other frosting uses: Tahini Currant Crispy Rice Bars (see recipe), frost honey cake, or as a spread on a sesame bagel.

Tahini Currant Crispy Rice Bars

YIELD: MAKES 1 8" × 8" PAN

1 batch Tahini Currant Frosting
1 cup Rice Chex
1–2 tablespoons sesame seeds

1. In a large bowl add Tahini Currant Frosting and Rice Chex. Mix until ingredients are evenly distributed; the mixture will be thick and sticky. Sprinkle with sesame seeds.

2. Press evenly into a parchment-lined 8" × 8" baking pan. Place in freezer to firm up for about 20 minutes. Remove from freezer and cut into squares.

PISTACHIO COCONUT FROSTING

YIELD: MAKES ABOUT 1½ CUPS

Pistachio Coconut Frosting has to be one of my favorite frostings on the planet—and it was a huge seller at the Dollop Cupcake Bar! Since you're going to want to eat this frosting by the spoonful, I've healthified it a bit so that you can dig in, pint-style, guilt free! This Pistachio Coconut Frosting is vegan, gluten-free, and going in my belly right now. Spread it on crackers, carrots, cupcakes, your tongue—seriously, you can't go wrong here!

½ cup whole salted dry-roasted pistachios
½ cup sweetened untoasted coconut (unsweetened works too,
    just add more coconut palm sugar to taste)
½ cup unrefined coconut oil, room temperature
½ cup coconut palm sugar
½ cup sweetened coconut

1. Preheat oven to 300°F. Grind pistachios to a fine powder in a food processor.

2. Spread ½ cup untoasted coconut evenly onto a parchment-lined baking sheet and bake for about 5–6 minutes, or until lightly browned. Remove from oven and let cool.

3. In the bowl of a stand mixer fitted with a paddle attachment, mix coconut oil until softened, about 3–5 minutes. Add pistachios, palm sugar, and all coconut, and continue mixing another 5 minutes until creamy and soft and ingredients are well combined. This is a thicker, chunkier frosting.

Extra Sweets!

Other frosting uses: Pistachio Coconut Cookie Thins (see recipe), a dip for wheat crackers, or as a replacement for the nut mixture in your favorite baklava recipe.

Pistachio Coconut Cookie Thins
with Pistachio Coconut Frosting

Pistachio Coconut Cookie Thins

YIELD: MAKES ABOUT 1 DOZEN COOKIES

1 batch Pistachio Coconut Frosting
1 egg white or egg white replacers
2 tablespoons dried cranberries

Preheat oven to 350°F. Combine Pistachio Coconut Frosting, egg whites or egg white replacers, and dried cranberries. Drop tablespoon-sized pieces of batter onto a parchment-lined baking sheet and bake for about 10–12 minutes. They will bake very flat. Allow to cool completely or they will break as you try to remove them from the parchment paper.

Honey Mustard Frosting

YIELD: FROSTS ABOUT 1½ DOZEN CUPCAKES

I don't attend many parties, but I have a party trick ready in case I do: balloon animals. Okay, more specifically, balloon poodles. I didn't make it past Balloon Animals 101. However, I have another party trick that's even more impressive . . . this deliciously unique Honey Mustard Frosting! Yes, people look at me like I'm nuts, but one bite of this slightly tangy yellow fluffiness and their shocked faces break into broad grins. Their smiles just widen when I hand them a balloon poodle to sweeten the deal.

½ cup unsalted butter, softened
1 cup powdered sugar
¼ teaspoon salt
5 teaspoons honey
6 teaspoons finely ground mustard powder

Mix butter in bowl of a stand mixer until softened. Add sugar, salt, honey, and mustard powder, and continue mixing until light and fluffy, about 5 minutes.

Extra Sweets!

Other frosting uses: Corn Dog Cupcakes (see recipe), pretzel dip, or chicken nugget dip.

Corn Dog Cupcakes with
Honey Mustard Frosting

Corn Dog Cupcakes

YIELD: MAKES ABOUT 14 CUPCAKES

½ cup unsalted butter
½ cup white sugar
2 eggs
1 cup buttermilk
½ teaspoon baking soda
1 cup cornmeal
1 cup flour
½ teaspoon salt
5 prebaked hot dogs or vegan dogs
1 batch Honey Mustard Frosting
14–20 pretzels, crushed

1. Preheat oven to 350°F. In small microwave-safe bowl, melt butter, then pour it into the bowl of a stand mixer and add sugar; mix until blended. Add eggs and continue mixing about 1 minute, until smooth. Add buttermilk, baking soda, cornmeal, flour, and salt, and mix until smooth.

2. Spray a cupcake pan with nonstick cooking spray and scoop in batter until about ¾ full. Slice hot dogs into ½" slices and put 3 hot dog slices in each cupcake, pressing down gently. Place in oven and bake for about 20–25 minutes or until the cupcakes feel slightly firm to the touch.

3. Remove from oven and allow to cool. Spread a thin layer of Honey Mustard Frosting on top, and top with crushed pretzels.

CHEDDAR BACON FROSTING

YIELD: MAKES DIP FOR ABOUT 5–6 DOZEN PRETZEL BITES

Cheesy, spicy, bacon frosting. Sounds pretty freakin' amazing, right? This frosting is a powerhouse of flavor and a guy's best friend! Serve it on game day with baked pretzels, or frost some cornbread and plate it next to a heaping pile of BBQ ribs. However you decide to use it, this spicy Cheddar Bacon Frosting will have the men on their knees and their buddies wishing their ladies were as killer as you.

8 ounces cream cheese, softened
8 ounces spreadable Cheddar cheese
¾ cup powdered sugar
⅛ teaspoon salt
½ teaspoon chipotle powder
¼ teaspoon cayenne powder
2 tablespoons bacon, cooked

In the bowl of a stand mixer fitted with a paddle attachment, beat cream cheese until smooth. Add Cheddar and continue mixing about 3 minutes, until smooth. Add sugar, salt, chipotle, cayenne, and bacon, and blend until smooth.

Extra Sweets!

Other frosting uses: Cheddar Beer-Boiled Pretzels (see recipe); frost cornbread; or dollop on potato skins, sprinkle with cheddar cheese, top with maple-smoked bacon, and bake until melted.

Cheddar Beer-Boiled Pretzels
with Cheddar Bacon Frosting

Cheddar Beer-Boiled Pretzels

YIELD: MAKES ABOUT 5–6 DOZEN PRETZELS

¾ cup warm water
½ tablespoon brown sugar
1 teaspoon salt
1 packet active dry yeast
2¼ cups flour
1 cup shredded Cheddar, divided in half

2 tablespoons unsalted butter, melted
2 bottles brown ale
1 egg yolk
2 teaspoons water
1 tablespoon kosher salt for garnish (optional)
1 batch Cheddar Bacon Frosting

1. In the bowl of a stand mixer fitted with the bread hook, add warm water, brown sugar, and salt. Pour yeast on top and allow to sit. In a separate bowl, whisk together flour and ½ cup shredded Cheddar cheese.

2. Once the water and yeast is foamy, after about 5 minutes, add the flour/cheese mixture and melted butter. Mix on low speed until just combined. Turn the mixer to medium and mix another 4–5 minutes until the dough is smooth. Remove the dough from the bowl, spray the bowl with nonstick cooking spray, replace the dough in the bowl, and cover tightly with plastic wrap; allow it to sit for 1 hour. The dough will double in size.

3. Once the dough has risen, divide it in half and roll one half flat to ⅛" thickness on a lightly floured surface. Repeat with the second half of dough, or you can wrap it in plastic and freeze for a later time. Use a standard shot glass upside down to cut circles in the dough. Set your dough circles aside.

4. Preheat oven to 350°F. In a large pot over medium heat, bring two bottles of brown ale to a boil. Drop the dough circles in, 4 or 5 at a time, and boil for about 30 seconds each. Remove from pot and place in the bottoms of a mini cupcake tin coated in nonstick cooking spray. Press the dough circles into cup shapes by pressing down in the bottom and up around the sides with a ⅛ teaspoon measuring spoon. In a small bowl, mix the egg yolk and 2 teaspoons water to make an egg wash. Lightly brush each pretzel with the egg wash, and sprinkle with remaining ½ cup Cheddar cheese and kosher salt, if desired.

5. Bake the pretzels in the cupcake tins for 10–12 minutes, until they start to brown. Remove from oven and serve immediately with the Cheddar Bacon Frosting in a side dish for dipping. Or, save your guests the dipping and scoop ½-teaspoon-sized dollops of Cheddar Bacon Frosting onto each pretzel bite. Leftover pretzels can be stored in a Ziploc bag in the fridge.

Cinnamon Whisky Buttercream

YIELD: FROSTS ABOUT 1½ DOZEN CUPCAKES

To really showcase the Monster Jam theme on my episode of Cupcake Wars, *I decided to create a fiery Cinnamon Whisky Buttercream to represent the sometimes catastrophic truck fires at monster truck rallies! I really didn't know much about trucks, but I knew enough about frosting to know that adding a dash of cinnamon and a splash of spicy whisky would leave a lasting impression on the judges. So I whipped cinnamon whisky into this glorious, speckled Cinnamon Whisky Buttercream and dolloped it atop my Strawberry Firebomb Cupcakes to take home the crown!*

1 cup unsalted butter, softened
1½ tablespoons cinnamon whisky
3¼ cups 10x powdered sugar
⅛ teaspoon salt
½ tablespoon ground cinnamon

Mix butter at room temperature in stand mixer with paddle until soft, about 3 minutes. Add cinnamon whisky and continue mixing for another minute. Slowly add powdered sugar and continue mixing about 3 minutes. Add salt and cinnamon, and continue mixing until light and fluffy, about 5 minutes. Scrape sides and bottom of bowl to ensure all ingredients are fully incorporated and distributed evenly and mix until light and creamy, another 2 minutes.

Extra Sweets!

Other frosting uses: Strawberry Firebomb Cupcakes (see recipe), vanilla wafer cinnamon whisky sandwiches, dolloped atop a shot of hot cinnamon whisky.

Strawberry Firebomb
Cupcakes with Cinnamon
Whisky Buttercream

Strawberry Firebomb Cupcakes

FOR CUPCAKES

½ cup milk
6 large egg whites
2¼ cups all-purpose flour
1¾ cups granulated sugar
1 teaspoon salt
1 teaspoon cayenne pepper
4 teaspoons baking powder
¾ cup unsalted butter, softened
1 cup strawberry purée
½ cup cinnamon whisky

FOR STRAWBERRY FLAMBÉ FILLING

YIELD: APPROXIMATELY 1 CUP

2 tablespoons unsalted butter
2 tablespoons brown sugar
1 cup strawberries, chopped
2 ounces cinnamon whisky

1. **For cupcakes:** Preheat oven to 350°F. Line a cupcake or muffin tin with 12 cupcake liners. In the bowl of an electric stand mixer with a paddle attachment, pour in milk and egg whites and mix until blended. In a separate bowl, mix flour, sugar, salt, cayenne pepper, and baking powder. Add butter and continue beating until mixture resembles moist crumbs. Add half of the milk mixture to the crumbs and beat at medium speed for 60–90 seconds. To the remaining half of the milk mixture, add the strawberry purée and mix with a whisk. Add this to the batter and beat for 30 seconds. Stop mixer and scrape sides of bowl, then beat for an additional 20 seconds. Add cinnamon whisky and blend. Spoon batter into cupcake tins until ¾ full. Bake for about 20–25 minutes or until a toothpick inserted in center comes out clean.

2. **For Strawberry Flambe Filling:** Melt butter with brown sugar in saucepan over medium heat. Add strawberries and continue cooking, about 2 minutes. Add cinnamon whisky and ignite with a lighter or match. Once the flame dies, remove from stove.

For Sugar Flames

1 cup sugar
¼ teaspoon lemon juice
Few drops red food coloring

For Topping

1 batch Cinnamon Whisky Buttercream
½ cup fireball candies, crushed

3. For Sugar Flames: Place sugar and lemon juice in a saucepan over medium heat and stir often until sugar melts and turns golden. Remove from heat and pour on silicone mat. Add a few drops red food coloring anywhere you like on the hot sugar. Use a toothpick to make a swirl design with the red food coloring. Let the sugar harden, flip tray upside down on a sheet tray, and whack into pieces.

4. To assemble: Cut a small hole in the center of a cupcake and fill with ½ tablespoon Strawberry Flambé Filling. Generously frost the top of each cupcake with Cinnamon Whisky Buttercream. Place broken pieces of Sugar Flames on top. This recipe goes great with Dollop's Firebomb frosting, too. Sprinkle crushed-up fireball candies on top for another fiery option.

Peanut Butter Granola with
Concord Grape Frosting

CONCORD GRAPE FROSTING

YIELD: MAKES ABOUT 1 CUP

One day I came upon a farmers' market and decided to stop, for nothing in particular. I'm so glad I did because that day I discovered the pure heavenly deliciousness of fresh Concord grapes. Buying a bundle, the first thing I did with them was rush to the kitchen to make this Concord Grape Frosting! It's like nothing you can even imagine—the juiciness, the freshness, the way the grapes burst through the creamy vanilla of the buttercream. Insane! If grapes are out of season, you can use preserves, but earmark this page and date your calendar for mid-September when the grapes are ripe for the picking. You won't want to miss this.

¼ cup butter, softened (can use vegan butter as well)
1 teaspoon vanilla
1¼ cups powdered sugar
7 teaspoons Concord grape preserves, or 4 or 5 fresh crushed Concord grapes

In the bowl of a stand mixer, whip butter with vanilla for about 2 minutes. Add sugar and Concord grape preserves and continuing mixing, about 5 minutes. Note: If using fresh Concord grapes, remove the skins and seeds and add the flesh to your frosting. The flesh of 4 or 5 grapes should be enough, but taste as you go. If you add too many, the frosting will start to separate, so be careful.

Extra Sweets!

Other frosting uses: Peanut Butter Granola (see recipe); mix ½ tablespoon each of frosting and peanut butter into plain Greek yogurt and top with walnuts; or for mini kebabs, on a toothpick place half a red grape, a small piece of blue cheese, and a spread of grape frosting, and roll in crushed pecans.

Peanut Butter Granola

YIELD: ABOUT 4–5 CUPS OF GRANOLA

2 cups natural crunchy peanut butter
2 cups gluten-free or regular oats
½ cup honey or agave nectar
½ cup dried cranberries
⅛ teaspoon coarse sea salt
1 batch Concord Grape Frosting

1. Preheat oven to 350°F. In a large bowl, mix all ingredients together until well blended. Press mixture firmly into a small square baking dish, about ½" thickness, and bake for 20–25 minutes.

2. Remove from oven and allow to cool. Scoop desired amount of granola in a bowl and top with a small scoop of Concord Grape Frosting. Stir and eat!

MAPLE BACON FROSTING

YIELD: MAKES ABOUT 1–2 CUPS

Why pour maple syrup on your waffles when you can spread freshly whipped Maple Bacon Frosting on them instead! Seriously, any time I order waffles at the local diner, they're served dripping with butter and soggy with syrup. Sorry syrup lovers, but ewww. This Maple Bacon Frosting is thick and rich like butter but smoky and sweet like maple syrup—the best of both worlds all whipped into one. Make several batches, store in airtight containers in the freezer, and pull out when that maple bacon craving strikes.

1 cup almond milk
2 cups brown sugar
⅛ teaspoon salt
¼ cup butter (can use vegan butter as well)

½ teaspoon pure vanilla extract
1 teaspoon maple extract
¼ cup bacon

1. In a saucepot over medium heat, stir almond milk with brown sugar and salt. Boil until it reaches 214°F on a candy thermometer, about 45 minutes. Stir only until it starts bubbling, then don't touch it. It will reduce to a brown caramel, becoming sticky and thick. Don't overcook or it will become hard.

2. Combine butter, vanilla extract, and maple extract in a medium bowl, then remove caramel mixture from stove and slowly pour over, whisking and breaking up the butter as you pour. Beat mixture on high with an electric whisk attachment for about 3 minutes, then let sit until gloss starts to fade, about 5 minutes, and mix in bacon. Whisk again for about 2 minutes and pour in airtight container to sit and thicken. Use immediately or store in freezer. Note: If freezing, microwave at 30-second intervals until it becomes soft and easy to stir again before using.

Extra Sweets!

Other frosting uses: Vanilla Buttermilk Waffles (see recipe), mix into home fries or hash browns, or frost cinnamon sugar cupcakes or snickerdoodles.

Vanilla Buttermilk Waffles

YIELD: MAKES 6 WAFFLES

2 eggs
2 cups flour
1¾ cups buttermilk
½ cup applesauce
1 tablespoon brown sugar, packed
4 teaspoons baking powder
1 teaspoon sea salt
1 teaspoon pure vanilla extract
½ teaspoon cinnamon
1 or 2 batches Maple Bacon Frosting, depending on
    how much you like to slather your waffles

1. Preheat waffle iron. Beat eggs in large bowl until fluffy. Beat in flour, buttermilk, apple-sauce, brown sugar, baking powder, sea salt, vanilla, and cinnamon, just until smooth.

2. Spray waffle iron with nonstick cooking spray. Pour mixture in batches, following your specific waffle iron instructions, onto hot waffle iron and cook until golden. Remove waffle from iron, plate, and coat with Maple Bacon Frosting!

Vanilla Buttermilk Waffles
with Maple Bacon Frosting

CONVERSION CHART

VOLUME CONVERSIONS

U.S. Volume Measure	Metric Equivalent
⅛ teaspoon	0.5 milliliter
¼ teaspoon	1 milliliter
½ teaspoon	2 milliliters
1 teaspoon	5 milliliters
½ tablespoon	7 milliliters
1 tablespoon (3 teaspoons)	15 milliliters
2 tablespoons (1 fluid ounce)	30 milliliters
¼ cup (4 tablespoons)	60 milliliters
⅓ cup	90 milliliters
½ cup (4 fluid ounces)	125 milliliters
⅔ cup	160 milliliters
¾ cup (6 fluid ounces)	180 milliliters
1 cup (16 tablespoons)	250 milliliters
1 pint (2 cups)	500 milliliters
1 quart (4 cups)	1 liter (about)

WEIGHT CONVERSIONS

U.S. Weight Measure	Metric Equivalent
½ ounce	15 grams
1 ounce	30 grams
2 ounces	60 grams
3 ounces	85 grams
¼ pound (4 ounces)	115 grams
½ pound (8 ounces)	225 grams
¾ pound (12 ounces)	340 grams
1 pound (16 ounces)	454 grams

OVEN TEMPERATURE CONVERSIONS

Degrees Fahrenheit	Degrees Celsius
200 degrees F	95 degrees C
250 degrees F	120 degrees C
275 degrees F	135 degrees C
300 degrees F	150 degrees C
325 degrees F	160 degrees C
350 degrees F	180 degrees C
375 degrees F	190 degrees C
400 degrees F	205 degrees C
425 degrees F	220 degrees C
450 degrees F	230 degrees C

BAKING PAN SIZES

U.S.	Metric
8 x 1½ inch round baking pan	20 x 4 cm cake tin
9 x 1½ inch round baking pan	23 x 3.5 cm cake tin
11 x 7 x 1½ inch baking pan	28 x 18 x 4 cm baking tin
13 x 9 x 2 inch baking pan	30 x 20 x 5 cm baking tin
2 quart rectangular baking dish	30 x 20 x 3 cm baking tin
15 x 10 x 2 inch baking pan	30 x 25 x 2 cm baking tin (Swiss roll tin)
9 inch pie plate	22 x 4 or 23 x 4 cm pie plate
7 or 8 inch springform pan	18 or 20 cm springform or loose bottom cake tin
9 x 5 x 3 inch loaf pan	23 x 13 x 7 cm or 2 lb narrow loaf or pâté tin
1½ quart casserole	1.5 liter casserole
2 quart casserole	2 liter casserole

INDEX

Note: Page numbers in **bold** indicate frosting recipes/photos and their respective baked goods. Page numbers in *italics* indicate recipes/photos of baked goods.

Alcoholic drinks, recipes with
about: types of, for recipes, 12
Bittersweet Chocolate, Clove, Beer, and Spicy Beer Caramel Cupcakes, *116–18*
Champagne Cake Bites with Raspberries, *99–100*
Cheddar Beer-Boiled Pretzels, *142–43*
Cinnamon Whisky Buttercream, **144–47**
Malbec Ganache Frosting, **89–91**
Margarita Crispy Rice Treats, *96–97*
Margarita Meringue Frosting, **95–97**
Strawberry Champagne Frosting, **98–100**
Strawberry-Frosted Limoncello "Shortcakes," *28–29*
Apple tarts, salted caramel, *31–32*

Bacon
Cashew Chocolate Bacon Bark, *131–32*
Cheddar Bacon Frosting, **141–43**
Maple Bacon Frosting, **151–53**
Bags, piping or Ziploc, 12
Baking pan sizes, 154
Baking tips, 14
Bananas
Bananas Foster Cupcake-Pancake Bites, *69–70*
Bananas Foster Frosting, **68–70**
Banana Split Cake Balls, *70, 72*

Basil, in Peach Basil Whipped Cream and Pancakes, **124–26**
Berries
Blackberry Brownies, *122–23*
Champagne Cake Bites with Raspberries, *99–100*
Chocolate Raspberry Pasta, *90–91*
Chocolate Strawberry Cream Cheese Frosting, **70–72**
Floating Strawberry Meringue Drop Cookies, *93–94*
Frosting Fruit Salad, *41–42*
Raspberry Buttercream, **51–53**
Strawberry Balsamic Goat Cheese Frosting, **118–20**
Strawberry Champagne Frosting, **98–100**
Strawberry Firebomb Cupcakes, *145–47*
Strawberry Flambé Filling, *146*
Strawberry-Frosted Limoncello "Shortcakes," *28–29*
Strawberry Frosting, **27–29**
Strawberry Meringue Frosting, **92–94**
Strawberry Spinach Cheesecakes, *119–20*
Sweet Potato Fries and Blueberry Ketchup Cupcakes, *59–61*
Tahini Currant Frosting, **132–34**
White Chocolate Blueberry Ganache, **108–10**

Blackberries. *See* Berries
Blending frosting, 14
Blueberries. *See* Berries
Book overview, 11
Brownie pans, 12
Brownies
Blackberry Brownies, *122–23*
Brownie Batter Frosting, **81–83**
Sriracha Brownies, *128–29*
Brown Sugar Frosting, **58–61**
Butter, 13
Buttercream
Chocolate Buttercream, **21–23**
Cinnamon Whisky Buttercream, **144–47**
Clove Buttercream, **114–17**
Peanut Butter Buttercream, **36–38**
Peppermint Buttercream, **46–48**
Raspberry Buttercream, **51–53**
Vanilla Buttercream, **18–20**

Cakes and cupcakes
about: baking, 14; *Cupcake Wars*, 9, 14–15, 36, 58, 114, 144; decorating, 14
Bananas Foster Cupcake-Pancake Bites, *69–70*
Banana Split Cake Balls, *70, 72*
Bittersweet Chocolate, Clove, Beer, and Spicy Beer Caramel Cupcakes, *116–18*
Champagne Cake Bites with Raspberries, *99–100*

Chocolate Cupcakes, *22–23*
Corn Dog Cupcakes, *139–40*
Mocha Upside-Down Cupcakes, *48, 50*
Red Velvet Cupcakes, *25–26*
Strawberry Firebomb Cupcakes, *145–47*
Strawberry-Frosted Limoncello
"Shortcakes," *28–29*
Sweet Potato Fries and Blueberry
Ketchup Cupcakes, *59–61*
Ultimate Dude Peanut Butter Cookie
Dough Cupcakes, *37–38*
Vanilla Cupcakes, *19–20*
Candy thermometer, 12
Caramel
Bittersweet Chocolate, Clove, Beer, and
Spicy Beer Caramel Cupcakes, *116–18*
Salted Caramel Frosting, **30–32**
Cardamom, in Orange Cardamom Icing,
111–13
Cashew Chocolate Bacon Bark, *131–32*
Cashew Sriracha Frosting, **127–29**
Champagne Cake Bites with Raspberries,
99–100
Cheese and cream cheese
Cheddar Bacon Frosting, **141–43**
Cheddar Beer-Boiled Pretzels, *142–43*
Chocolate Strawberry Cream Cheese
Frosting, **70–72**
Cream Cheese Frosting, **24–26**
Honey Brie Frosting, **105–7**
Pumpkin Spice Cream Cheese Frosting,
73–75
Strawberry Balsamic Goat Cheese
Frosting, **118–20**
Strawberry Spinach Cheesecakes,
119–20
Chocolate
Bittersweet Chocolate, Clove, Beer, and
Spicy Beer Caramel Cupcakes, *116–18*
Brownie Batter Frosting, **81–83**
Cashew Chocolate Bacon Bark, *131–32*

Chocolate Buttercream, **21–23**
Chocolate Chip Cookie Wafers, *62, 64*
Chocolate Chipotle Frosted Nachos
with Chili, *86, 88*
Chocolate Chipotle Frosting, **86–88**
Chocolate Cupcakes, *22–23*
Chocolate Raspberry Pasta, *90–91*
Chocolate Strawberry Cream Cheese
Frosting, **70–72**
Cookies and Cream Frosting, **42–45**
Cookies and Cream Ice Cream Trifle,
42, 44–45
Fondant-Covered Chocolate Chip
Cookie Tires, *39*
Juniper Chocolate Frosting, **121–23**
Mint Chocolate Chip Frosting, **33–35**
Mint Chocolate Cookie Trifle, *34–35*
Mocha Frosting, **48–50**
Mocha Upside-Down Cupcakes, *48, 50*
Salted Triple Chocolate Brownie Batter
Cookies, *82–83*
S'more Frosting, **54–56**
S'more Push-Pop Parfaits, *55–56*
Toffee Ganache Frosting, **76–78**
Ultimate Dude Peanut Butter Cookie
Dough Cupcakes, *37–38*
White Chocolate Blueberry Ganache,
108–10
Cinnamon Whisky Buttercream, **144–47**
Citrus
Frosting Fruit Salad, *41–42*
Lavender Orange Biscotti, *103–4*
Lavender Orange Frosting, **102–4**
Lemon Glaze Frosting, **40–42**
Orange Cardamom Icing, **111–13**
Orange Cut-Out Cookies, *112–13*
Strawberry-Frosted Limoncello
"Shortcakes," *28–29*
Classics, 17–56
about: overview of, 17
Chocolate Buttercream, **21–23**

Chocolate Cupcakes, *22–23*
Cookies and Cream Frosting, **42–45**
Cookies and Cream Ice Cream Trifle,
42, 44–45
Cream Cheese Frosting, **24–26**
Frosting Fruit Salad, *41–42*
Lemon Glaze Frosting, **40–42**
Mint Chocolate Chip Frosting, **33–35**
Mint Chocolate Cookie Trifle, *34–35*
Mocha Frosting, **48–50**
Mocha Upside-Down Cupcakes, *48, 50*
Peanut Butter Buttercream, **36–38**
Peppermint Buttercream, **46–48**
Peppermint Cookie Cups with
Peppermint Ice Cream, *47–48*
Raspberry Buttercream, **51–53**
Red Velvet Cupcakes, *25–26*
Salted Caramel Apple Tarts, *31–32*
Salted Caramel Frosting, **30–32**
S'more Frosting, **54–56**
S'more Push-Pop Parfaits, *55–56*
Spinach "Salad," *52–53*
Strawberry-Frosted Limoncello
"Shortcakes," *28–29*
Strawberry Frosting, **27–29**
Ultimate Dude Peanut Butter Cookie
Dough Cupcakes, *37–38*
Vanilla Buttercream, **18–20**
Vanilla Cupcakes, *19–20*
Clove Buttercream, **114–17**
Coconut
Coconut Almond Frosting, **130–32**
Pistachio Coconut Cookie Thins, *136–37*
Pistachio Coconut Frosting, **135–37**
Coffee
Coffee Toffee Ganache Frosting
Truffles, *77–78*
Hazelnut Coffee Frosting, **78–80**
Mocha Frosting, **48–50**
Mocha Upside-Down Cupcakes, *48, 50*
Vanilla Hazelnut Coffee Pudding, *78, 80*

Concord Grape Frosting, **148–50**
Conversion chart, 154
Cookie dough
    Cookie Dough Frosting, **62–64**
    Ultimate Dude Peanut Butter Cookie
        Dough Cupcakes, *37–38*
Cookies. *See also* Brownies; Rice treats
    Chocolate Chip Cookie Wafers, *62, 64*
    Cookies and Cream Frosting, **42–45**
    Cookies and Cream Ice Cream Trifle,
        42, 44–45
    Floating Strawberry Meringue Drop
        Cookies, *93–94*
    Lavender Orange Biscotti, *103–4*
    Mint Chocolate Cookie Trifle, *34–35*
    Orange Cut-Out Cookies, *112–13*
    Pear Cookies, *109–10*
    Peppermint Cookie Cups with
        Peppermint Ice Cream, *47–48*
    Pistachio Coconut Cookie Thins, *136–37*
    Rosemary Sea Salt Shortbreads with
        Fig, *106–7*
    Salted Triple Chocolate Brownie Batter
        Cookies, *82–83*
Cookie sheets, 12
Cooling racks, 12
Corn
    Corn Dog Cupcakes, *139–40*
    Frosted Popcorn, *66–67*
Crazy recipes, 101–53
    about: overview of, 101
    Bittersweet Chocolate, Clove, Beer, and
        Spicy Beer Caramel Cupcakes, *116–18*
    Blackberry Brownies, *122–23*
    Cashew Chocolate Bacon Bark, *131–32*
    Cashew Sriracha Frosting, **127–29**
    Cheddar Bacon Frosting, **141–43**
    Cheddar Beer-Boiled Pretzels, *142–43*
    Cinnamon Whisky Buttercream, **144–47**
    Clove Buttercream, **114–17**
    Coconut Almond Frosting, **130–32**

Concord Grape Frosting, **148–50**
Corn Dog Cupcakes, *139–40*
Honey Brie Frosting, **105–7**
Honey Mustard Frosting, **138–40**
Juniper Chocolate Frosting, **121–23**
Lavender Orange Biscotti, *103–4*
Lavender Orange Frosting, **102–4**
Maple Bacon Frosting, **151–53**
Orange Cardamom Icing, **111–13**
Orange Cut-Out Cookies, *112–13*
Peach Basil Pancakes, *125–26*
Peach Basil Whipped Cream, **124–26**
Peanut Butter Granola, *150*
Peanut Butter Granola with Concord
    Grape Frosting, *148*
Pear Cookies, *109–10*
Pistachio Coconut Cookie Thins, *136–37*
Pistachio Coconut Frosting, **135–37**
Rosemary Sea Salt Shortbreads with
    Fig, *106–7*
Sriracha Brownies, *128–29*
Strawberry Balsamic Goat Cheese
    Frosting, **118–20**
Strawberry Firebomb Cupcakes, *145–47*
Strawberry Spinach Cheesecakes,
    119–20
Tahini Currant Crispy Rice Bars, *132, 134*
Tahini Currant Frosting, **132–34**
Vanilla Buttermilk Waffles, *152–53*
White Chocolate Blueberry Ganache,
    108–10
Cupcakes. *See* Cakes and cupcakes
Cupcake Wars (CW) recipes
    about, 9, 14–15
    Bittersweet Chocolate, Clove, Beer, and
        Spicy Beer Caramel Cupcakes, *116–18*
    Brown Sugar Frosting, **58–61**
    Cinnamon Whisky Buttercream, **144–47**
    Clove Buttercream, **114–17**
    Peanut Butter Buttercream, **36–38**
    Strawberry Firebomb Cupcakes, *145–47*

    Sweet Potato Fries and Blueberry
        Ketchup Cupcakes, *59–61*
    Ultimate Dude Peanut Butter Cookie
        Dough Cupcakes, *37–38*
Custard dishes, 12
CW. *See Cupcake Wars* (CW) recipes

Decorating tips, 14
Dishes, for frosting, 12, 13

Figs, in Rosemary Sea Salt Shortbreads
    with Fig, *106–7*
Floating Strawberry Meringue Drop
    Cookies, *93–94*
Fondant
    about, 14
    Fondant-Covered Chocolate Chip
        Cookie Tires, *39*
Food processor, 12
Forks, 12
Frosted Popcorn, *66–67*
Frosting, making
    author perspective on, 8–9
    book overview, 11
    decorating after, 14
    ingredients for recipes, 13. *See also
        specific main ingredients*
    storing after, 14
    styles of frosting and, 13
    techniques for, 14
    tools and supplies for, 12–13
    yields, 15. *See also specific recipes*
Frosting Fruit Salad, *41–42*
Fruit salad, frosting, *41–42*

Ganache
    Malbec Ganache Frosting, **89–91**
    Toffee Ganache Frosting, **76–78**
    White Chocolate Blueberry Ganache,
        108–10
Gingersnap Stout Frosting, **84–86**

Gingersnap Stout Pie, *85–86*
Granola, peanut butter, *148, 150*
Grape frosting, peanut butter granola and, **148–50**

Hazelnut Coffee Frosting, **78–80**
Honey Brie Frosting, **105–7**
Honey Mustard Frosting, **138–40**

Ice cream
    Cookies and Cream Ice Cream Trifle, *42, 44–45*
    Peppermint Cookie Cups with Peppermint Ice Cream, *47–48*
Ice cream scoops, *12*
Ingredients for recipes, *13. See also specific main ingredients*

Juniper Chocolate Frosting, **121–23**

Knives, *12*

Lavender Orange Biscotti, *103–4*
Lavender Orange Frosting, **102–4**
Lemon. *See* Citrus

Malbec Ganache Frosting, **89–91**
Maple Bacon Frosting, **151–53**
Margarita Crispy Rice Treats, *96–97*
Margarita Meringue Frosting, **95–97**
Measurement conversion chart, *154*
Measuring cups and spoons, *12*
Meringues
    Floating Strawberry Meringue Drop Cookies, *93–94*
    Margarita Meringue Frosting, **95–97**
    Strawberry Meringue Frosting, **92–94**
Metric conversion chart, *154*
Mint
    Mint Chocolate Chip Frosting, **33–35**
    Peppermint Buttercream, **46–48**

Peppermint Cookie Cups with Peppermint Ice Cream, *47–48*
Mixer, *13*
Mocha Frosting, **48–50**
Mocha Upside-Down Cupcakes, *48, 50*
Music, *12*
Mustard, in Honey Mustard Frosting, **138–40**

Nachos, chocolate chipotle frosted with chili, *86, 88*
Nonstick cooking spray, *12*
Nuts and seeds
    Cashew Chocolate Bacon Bark, *131–32*
    Cashew Sriracha Frosting, **127–29**
    Coconut Almond Frosting, **130–32**
    Hazelnut Coffee Frosting, **78–80**
    Peanut Butter Buttercream, **36–38**
    Peanut Butter Granola, *150*
    Peanut Butter Granola with Concord Grape Frosting, *148*
    Pistachio Coconut Cookie Thins, *136–37*
    Pistachio Coconut Frosting, **135–37**
    Pumpkin Spice Pizzas, *74–75*
    Spinach "Salad," *52–53*
    Ultimate Dude Peanut Butter Cookie Dough Cupcakes, *37–38*
    Vanilla Hazelnut Coffee Pudding, *78, 80*

Orange. *See* Citrus
Oven temperature conversions, *154*

Pancakes and waffles
    Bananas Foster Cupcake-Pancake Bites, *69–70*
    Peach Basil Pancakes, *125–26*
    Vanilla Buttermilk Waffles, *152–53*
Pans, *12, 154*
Paper, parchment and wax, *12*
Parchment paper, *12*
Pasta, chocolate raspberry, *90–91*

Peach Basil Pancakes, *125–26*
Peach Basil Whipped Cream, **124–26**
Peanut Butter Buttercream, **36–38**
Peanut Butter Granola with Concord Grape Frosting, *148*
Pear Cookies, *109–10*
Peppermint. *See* Mint
Pie pans, *12*
Pies and tarts
    Gingersnap Stout Pie, *85–86*
    Salted Caramel Apple Tarts, *31–32*
    Strawberry Spinach Cheesecakes, *119–20*
Piping bags, *12*
Pistachio Coconut Cookie Thins, *136–37*
Pistachio Coconut Frosting, **135–37**
Pizzas, pumpkin spice, *74–75*
Popcorn, frosted, *66–67*
Powdered sugar, *13*
Pretzels, cheddar beer-boiled, *142–43*
Pumpkin Spice Cream Cheese Frosting, **73–75**
Pumpkin Spice Pizzas, *74–75*
Push-pop containers, *12*
Push-pop parfait, s'more, *55–56*

Ramekins, *12*
Recipes
    decorating tips, *14*
    ingredients for, *13. See also specific main ingredients*
    techniques for, *14*
    tools and supplies for, *12–13*
    yields, *15. See also specific recipes*
Red Velvet Cupcakes, *25–26*
Rice treats
    Margarita Crispy Rice Treats, *96–97*
    Tahini Currant Crispy Rice Bars, *132, 134*
Rosemary Sea Salt Shortbreads with Fig, *106–7*

"Salad," spinach, *52–53*
Salt, *13–14*
Salted Caramel Apple Tarts, *31–32*
Salted Caramel Frosting, **30–32**
Salted Triple Chocolate Brownie Batter Cookies, *82–83*
Scissors, *12*
"Shortcakes," strawberry-frosted limoncello, *28–29*
S'more Frosting, **54–56**
S'more Push-Pop Parfaits, *55–56*
Spatulas, *12*
Spinach
    Spinach "Salad," *52–53*
    Strawberry Spinach Cheesecakes, *119–20*
Spoons, *12*
Sriracha Brownies, *128–29*
Stand mixer, *13*
Storing frosting, *14*
Strawberries. *See* Berries
Styles of frosting, *13*
Sugar, powdered, *13*
Sugar, sweetness and, *14–15*
Supplies and tools, *12–13*
Sweetness levels, *14–15*
Sweet Potato Fries and Blueberry Ketchup Cupcakes, *59–61*

Tahini Currant Crispy Rice Bars, *132, 134*
Tahini Currant Frosting, **132–34**
Tarts, salted caramel apple, *31–32*
Techniques, *14.* *See also* Frosting, making
Temperature conversions, *154*
Thermometer, candy, *12*
Toffee
    Frosted Popcorn, *66–67*
    Toffee Ganache Frosting, **76–78**
    Toffee Honey Frosting, **65–67**
Tools and supplies, *12–13*
Toothpicks, *13*

Trifles
    about: dishes for, *13*
    Cookies and Cream Ice Cream Trifle, *42, 44–45*
    Mint Chocolate Cookie Trifle, *34–35*
Truffles, coffee toffee ganache frosting, *77–78*
Twist, recipes with a. *See* With a twist

Ultimate Dude Peanut Butter Cookie Dough Cupcakes, *37–38*

Vanilla
    Vanilla Buttercream, **18–20**
    Vanilla Buttermilk Waffles, *152–53*
    Vanilla Cupcakes, *19–20*
    Vanilla Hazelnut Coffee Pudding, *78, 80*
Volume conversions, *154*

Waffles, vanilla buttermilk, *152–53*
Wax paper, *12*
Weight conversions, *154*
Whipped cream, peach basil, **124–26**
Whipping frosting, *14*
White Chocolate Blueberry Ganache, **108–10**
With a twist, *57–100*
    about: overview of, *57*
    Bananas Foster Cupcake-Pancake Bites, *69–70*
    Bananas Foster Frosting, **68–70**
    Banana Split Cake Balls, *70, 72*
    Brownie Batter Frosting, **81–83**
    Brown Sugar Frosting, **58–61**
    Champagne Cake Bites with Raspberries, *99–100*
    Chocolate Chip Cookie Wafers, *62, 64*
    Chocolate Chipotle Frosted Nachos with Chili, *86, 88*
    Chocolate Chipotle Frosting, **86–88**
    Chocolate Raspberry Pasta, *90–91*

    Chocolate Strawberry Cream Cheese Frosting, **70–72**
    Coffee Toffee Ganache Frosting Truffles, *77–78*
    Cookie Dough Frosting, **62–64**
    Floating Strawberry Meringue Drop Cookies, *93–94*
    Frosted Popcorn, *66–67*
    Gingersnap Stout Frosting, **84–86**
    Gingersnap Stout Pie, *85–86*
    Hazelnut Coffee Frosting, **78–80**
    Malbec Ganache Frosting, **89–91**
    Margarita Crispy Rice Treats, *96–97*
    Margarita Meringue Frosting, **95–97**
    Pumpkin Spice Cream Cheese Frosting, **73–75**
    Pumpkin Spice Pizzas, *74–75*
    Salted Triple Chocolate Brownie Batter Cookies, *82–83*
    Strawberry Champagne Frosting, **98–100**
    Strawberry Meringue Frosting, **92–94**
    Sweet Potato Fries and Blueberry Ketchup Cupcakes, *59–61*
    Toffee Ganache Frosting, **76–78**
    Toffee Honey Frosting, **65–67**
    Vanilla Hazelnut Coffee Pudding, *78, 80*

Yields, *15. See also specific recipes*

Ziploc bags, *12*

ABOUT THE AUTHOR

Heather "Cupcakes" Saffer

is the president and founder of Dollop Gourmet. Over the past five years she has perfected her frosting recipes, using them to frost cupcakes for thousands of men, women, and children at her former cupcake bar, Dollop Gourmet Cupcake Creations, and at events across the country. A winner of Food Network's *Cupcake Wars*, public speaker, and social media lover, Heather pushes the boundaries on what can be done with frosting (and life), and brings her infectious smile and antics online at heathersaffer.com. For a regular glimpse into Heather's kitchen, life, and hilarious insights, check out her vlog on YouTube. Find her everywhere as @HeatherCupcakes.